The
Purposeful
Leader

THE PURPOSEFUL LEADER

How Multi-Dimensional Thinking Shapes Leadership in a World That Won't Sit Still

Neil C. Tarallo

Published by Game Changer Publishing

Paperback ISBN: 978-1-968250-30-0

Hardcover ISBN: 978-1-968250-31-7

Digital ISBN: 978-1-968250-32-4

GC | GAME CHANGER
PUBLISHING

www.GameChangerPublishing.com

For my wife Paula, the causal to my effectual.
Your clarity shapes my direction and your presence anchors my path.

To my son Dominic, who moves without waiting for a map and reminds me,
with each step, that I still have places to go.

To my mom and dad. One of you told me I could, the other showed me how.

And to all of my students, you have been the rocks that shaped
the course of my work and the depth of my thinking

READ THIS FIRST

Step Into Multi-Dimensional Leadership
Thank you for reading *The Purposeful Leader*.
Download your free exclusive tools, including the NOVA-U
Framework, to help you bring these ideas to life.

Scan the QR code, no obligation, just actionable resources.

If you're interested in becoming a client and developing
multi-dimensional leadership skills for yourself or your
team, please use the link provided with your download.

Scan the QR Code Here:

ADVANCE PRAISE FOR NEIL C. TARALLO

"As someone helping senior leaders navigate uncertainty across industries —from finance to healthcare to government—I found *The Purposeful Leader* to be both resonant and essential. The emphasis on effectual reasoning and translation mirrors what we teach: that resilience is built not on rigid plans, but on purposeful action, iteration, and meaning-making."

— John Kallelil, CEO, XED

"Studying effectual thinking with Neil changed the course of my life. The concepts in this book gave me clarity on navigating uncertainty and empowered me to act with greater agency. These teachings have helped me start companies, effectively lead in stressful situations, and ultimately build a career and life that feel true to who I am."

— Sean Corcoran, Software Engineer, Entrepreneur

"There are so many ways that Neil Tarallo contributes to better leadership in this book. Whether you're a start-up entrepreneur or a Fortune 500 CEO, you will get something out of reading *The Purposeful Leader*. I'm always looking for ways to better my leadership style, and this does that."

— Chris Roush, Assistant VP of Strategic Partnerships, Elon University
Author of *The Future of Business Journalism:*
Why it Matters for Wall Street and Main Street

"I love the framework Neil presents in this book. Neil was one of the first people who taught me that you can still adopt an entrepreneurial mindset even if you work in a large company. This book gets at the heart of what that truly means—all organizations should embrace the idea of effectual thinking."

— Zach Demuth, Global Head, Hotels Research, JLL

"As one of Neil's students, I lived this thinking before I had words for it. Now I lead with it every day. A modern guide for navigating leadership when there's no map. Essential reading."

— Chris Kirby, Founder & CEO, Ithaca Hummus

"*The Purposeful Leader* goes well beyond academic insight; it's a strategic and grounded guide to navigating the ever-changing realities of leadership in both business and life. Through real-world examples, Neil captures what it truly means to lead when things don't go as planned. This should be required reading for anyone in a leadership role."

— Jason Spillerman, Owner, Vibrant Development Group

"*The Purposeful Leader* is one of those books that makes you stop and think *Finally, someone gets it*. Neil Tarallo doesn't just talk about leadership in theory ... he's lived it, and it shows. He puts words to the things a lot of us have felt but didn't know how to explain, especially when the usual tools of planning and control fall short. The way he frames multi-dimensional leadership really stuck with me ... practical, human, and flexible! It's not your typical leadership book, and that's exactly why it works. If you've ever felt like you lead differently than what the textbooks say, this one will hit home!"

— Marisa Sergi, CEO @ L'uva Bella Winery, CRO The Brew Kettle

The
Purposeful
Leader

HOW MULTI-DIMENSIONAL THINKING
SHAPES LEADERSHIP IN A WORLD
THAT WON'T SIT STILL

Neil C. Tarallo

AUTHOR'S NOTE

I didn't set out to write a book. I was just trying to make sense of things and to understand how leadership works when the world won't sit still.

For most of my life, I've lived in two overlapping spaces, one shaped by the work of doing, and the other shaped by the questions that come up while trying to do it well. I've built things. Started things. Taught others how to do the same.

But underneath it all, I've been trying to figure out what actually makes leadership work. Not just in theory. In practice. In messy, real environments where things don't always line up.

I've been an entrepreneur for most of my life. I started early—earlier than I understood what it really meant. I didn't have words for what I was doing. I just knew I saw things a certain way and made decisions based on what was in front of me. What I could reach. What I could afford to try.

At the time, it didn't feel like anything special. It felt like survival. Like common sense. And more often than not, it felt like something I had to explain. Or justify. Because it didn't always look the way people expected leadership to look.

But I wasn't alone in that. I grew up around people who lived this way. Entrepreneurs in my community, men and women who didn't talk much about frameworks or decision science but who modeled something steady and real. They made choices by feel. They adjusted without waiting for permission. They built what they could, starting with what was in their hands. I didn't think of it as a method back then. It was just the way people got things done. The way problems got solved. The way work moved forward.

My father was one of those people. He was the kind of entrepreneur who never needed to say the word. He just lived it. He understood the value of relationships, the weight of reputation, and the rhythm of risk that came with trying to create something useful. I didn't realize at the time how much I was learning from him by watching how he moved, how he made decisions, how he stayed grounded even when the next step wasn't clear.

But later, when I began to study these things more formally, I saw it. What I had been witnessing all along was "effectual logic" as a lived practice. And my father, more than anyone, helped me see that. He didn't explain it in academic terms. He just helped me make sense of what I was already doing, and he did it with a kind of quiet confidence that stays with me even now.

Years later, when I began teaching, I started to find language for those instincts. I began reading more. Paying attention to how others were thinking about uncertainty. About risk. About how decisions actually get made in the absence of a roadmap.

That's when I came across a way of thinking that finally made sense to me. It was called "effectual thinking." It is a logic used by experienced entrepreneurs that starts with what you have and builds from there rather than chasing a fixed goal. It was the first thing I'd read that reflected how I'd been moving through the world as an entrepreneur and as someone trying to lead inside systems that didn't always feel built for motion. It didn't just offer insight. It gave me a sense of recognition. It helped me understand what I'd been doing and why it mattered.

That was the catalyst.

Over time, my teaching environment helped those ideas grow. I'm not a researcher. I'm a practitioner. My work, then and now, has been about bridging the gap; taking what the research tells us and translating it into something people can use. Something that lands inside a conversation. Or a boardroom. Or a hard decision.

The classroom became a laboratory for this. My students, especially over the last decade, have been thinking out loud with me. Pushing back. Asking better questions. The ones that stay with you. The ones that don't go away when the course ends.

More than once, a student would stop by after class and say something like, "Why isn't this required?" Or, "Why did it take me this long to hear someone explain it this way?" I didn't always have a good answer. But those conversations stuck. And they pushed me to keep going.

Executive education clients added another layer. They weren't just interested in concepts. They wanted to see how this way of thinking could show up in practice. They asked for frameworks. Language. Ways to bring the work into their teams. Somewhere in those conversations, the name "multi-dimensional leadership" started to take hold as a way to point toward the kind of leadership that actually shows up when the work is complex, and the path isn't clear.

So that's what this book is. Not a manual. Not a model. But a way of thinking through what it means to lead when the answers aren't obvious, and the choices carry weight. A way to recognize the dimensions that show up when the work is layered. Strategic, yes, but also relational. Analytical, but also ethical. Practical, but also personal.

None of this came from a single moment. It came from a life lived. From dots collected over time. From jobs and conversations and missteps. From years of standing in rooms with people trying to make sense of hard things. From watching them hold tension, ask better questions, and keep going even when the picture wasn't clear.

This book is for them. And maybe for you, too. If you've ever felt like your way of leading didn't quite fit the mold, or if you've been carrying something you didn't know how to name, this is the language I've found.

Each chapter in this book is shaped around three parts. The first explores a leadership concept that often gets overlooked in traditional models but becomes essential when uncertainty is high and the path isn't clear.

The second is a story, usually drawn from my own lived experience. These aren't case studies or polished examples. They're moments where something meaningful took shape, often before I had language for it.

The third is where the work begins to turn outward. A short section that asks how these ideas might show up across three dimensions of your life: in the systems you help lead, in the direction of your career, and in the way you navigate your life as a whole.

That story and its application aren't about clarity for its own sake. They're meant to support the kind of leadership this book is about. Multi-dimensional. Lived. And always in motion.

I hope it helps.

CONTENTS

BECOMING A MULTI-DIMENSIONAL LEADER

I don't think I would have been able to name it back then. It was just a sense I had, a pattern I started to notice. Something was missing from how leadership was being taught and even more from how it was being lived. Not missing like an oversight or a forgotten piece of advice, but something quieter. A way of moving. A way of thinking that didn't show up in the handbooks or the frameworks, but seemed to matter deeply when things got complicated.

It took me a while to realize what I was seeing. And even longer to understand how much it shaped the leaders I worked with, and the one I was trying to become.

We spend a lot of time teaching leaders how to plan and execute. How to set goals and measure progress. How to control risk and manage performance. Those tools matter, of course. In a stable world, they can make a big difference, but the world hasn't felt stable for a while now, and certainly not in the ways that count.

And when things shift, that is when the environment gets messy or unpredictable. It's those familiar tools that don't always hold up. That's when you start to feel the absence of something else. A different kind of capability. One that's harder to define, but deeply important. The ability to keep leading even when you don't know what's coming. To act when the picture isn't clear. To begin without waiting for the answers.

I think of it now as a kind of inner flexibility. A way of holding space for uncertainty without freezing up. A way of engaging with complexity that doesn't rely on having everything mapped out ahead of time.

That's not something most leaders are trained for. It doesn't show up in performance reviews. It's not often rewarded in systems that are built around efficiency. But it's the thing that shows up when the plan breaks. When the pressure is high, and the road ahead doesn't look like any road you've walked before.

I've come to call it multi-dimensional leadership because it asks us to bring more of ourselves into how we lead. Not just the strategic thinker. Not just the planner. But also the experimenter. The translator. The person who can see what's shifting and respond in ways that create possibility and not just maintain control.

I want to be clear about something, though. This isn't about replacing what leaders already know. It's not about abandoning planning, analysis, or discipline. It's about adding something that's often left out. Expanding the range of what leaders can do, and how they think. It's about making room for a different kind of intelligence, one that's been there all along, but hasn't always been named or encouraged.

And it's also about something else. Something quieter. It's about helping others do the same.

Because leadership isn't just about how we move through the world. It's also about how we create space for others to move. To take risks. To respond to change. To lead in ways that don't always follow the script.

That's where this book begins: with a way of noticing. It's less a formula or model, and more a way of paying attention. A way of naming what's often overlooked, and starting to build from there.

THE MISSING LINK

There is an element in leadership that often goes unacknowledged. You will not find it listed in MBA syllabi, corporate handbooks, or strategic planning frameworks. It tends to remain in the background, hard to name, until it becomes noticeably absent. Once you become aware of it, you can see how often it is missing and how much it matters.

This quiet absence is the element I want to name. It is the ability to think and act in ways that remain effective even when clarity is unavailable. It does not replace what leaders already know. It expands it.

What's missing is not simply a set of skills or strategies. What's missing is the capacity for generative leadership under uncertainty. Across organizations, communities, and even personal lives, we have deprioritized the ability to act without full information, to begin without guarantees, and to respond in ways that create and not just protect value.

We have spent years building systems that reward predictability. We teach children to answer correctly rather than ask better questions. We celebrate efficiency over emergence. We invest in technologies that automate control but underinvest in the human capabilities that allow people to navigate the unexpected.

What's missing is the practice of leadership as a creative, adaptive, and relational act. A way of being in the world that goes beyond positional authority or tactical execution. It's the kind of leadership that shows up when a business model fails, when the path forward isn't in the playbook, or when the people around you are looking for direction but no map exists.

In this broader sense, what's missing is the development of constructive agency. The belief and behavior that says: "I may not know what will happen next, but I can engage anyway. I can move thoughtfully with what I do have and shape what comes."

And just as importantly, what's missing is the ability to help others do the same.

MULTI-DIMENSIONAL LEADERSHIP COMPASS

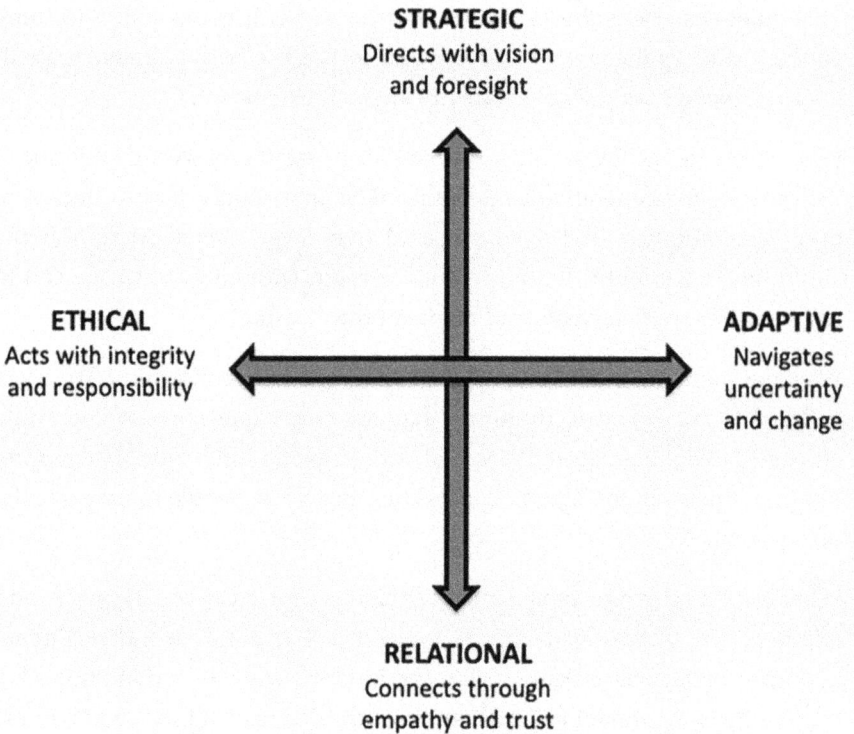

STRATEGIC
Directs with vision
and foresight

ETHICAL
Acts with integrity
and responsibility

ADAPTIVE
Navigates
uncertainty
and change

RELATIONAL
Connects through
empathy and trust

Figure 1: This compass illustrates the four essential orientations of multi-dimensional leadership. The model serves as both a diagnostic and developmental tool for balanced, context-aware leadership.

INTERPRETING THE COMPASS

This compass represents the foundational premise of Chapter 1: that effective leadership in uncertain environments requires more than execution and strategy—it demands a multi-dimensional orientation. Each directional axis reflects a dimension of leadership that can be activated based on what the moment requires:

- Strategic: The capacity to define vision, allocate resources, and drive intentional direction.

- Adaptive: The flexibility to act under uncertainty, adjust course, and learn in motion.

- Relational: The emotional and interpersonal intelligence to build trust and empower others.

- Ethical: The grounding in values, responsibility, and integrity that shapes long-term impact.

What makes this model powerful is not the presence of each trait, but the leader's ability to move fluidly between them and to adapt their stance based on shifting conditions while staying grounded in purpose. In this sense, the compass is not just descriptive; it's a directional tool and a way to calibrate leadership in motion.

Wherever a leader finds themselves navigating complexity, guiding others through ambiguity, or holding firm in ethical dilemmas, this compass offers a reminder: leadership is not one thing. It is a practiced, adaptive posture. Always in motion. Always in relationship with the world it is trying to move.

REFLECTION PROMPT

Think about a recent leadership moment; large or small, where you had to make a decision, guide a team, or respond to uncertainty.

- Which dimension of the compass did you rely on most: Strategic, Adaptive, Relational, or Ethical?

- Was there another dimension you might have overlooked that could have helped?

- How might your leadership shift if you treated these four directions as a dynamic system rather than static traits?

Too often, we assume this kind of leadership is intuitive or innate. But it isn't. It must be cultivated. It requires different muscles than those built by managing performance or scaling known systems. It asks us to be both more rigorous and more imaginative to hold ambiguity without losing accountability.

And at a societal level, the consequences of this absence are showing. In public discourse, we see polarization where translation is needed. In education, we see students trained to deliver answers but underprepared to navigate uncertainty. In organizations, we see leaders excelling in stable conditions but struggling to adapt when the ground shifts.

This is not a failure of intelligence or effort. It is a failure of design, a gap in what we prepare people to handle. And that gap is now widening as the world grows more complex, fast-moving, and interdependent.

"Effectual reasoning" is one part of the solution. Translation is another. The larger imperative is to reimagine leadership by shifting the focus from what we do when things are going well, to how we move when what's ahead is still unclear.

Over the past twenty years, I have worked with a wide range of people and organizations. From global companies to startups, from transforming mid-sized firms to family businesses adapting to new realities. Despite their differences, a common pattern has emerged. Leaders are finding it difficult to navigate increasingly complex and uncertain environments.

They bring ability, insight, and discipline. Many are successful professionals who have worked hard to master established methods of leadership: goal setting, performance systems, structured planning, and operational efficiency.

In stable settings, these methods have proven their value. Studies in organizational behavior and management science confirm that they deliver consistent results when the landscape is predictable.

But the context has changed. The world today is shaped by intersecting forces such as technological change, shifting expectations, and unpredictable global events. In many industries, the pace of change has acceler- ated beyond the reach of conventional planning tools. Leaders are being asked to respond to problems that do not resemble anything they have prepared for. These challenges are not just new in content. They are different in form.

In such situations, the usual tools begin to feel less useful. The methods leaders have relied on still have value, but something else is needed along- side them. The gap becomes visible less as a failure and more as a shift in what the moment demands. Some problems are not waiting for better control. They are waiting for a different kind of engagement.

"Causal reasoning" plays a dominant role in how most leadership systems are structured. It begins with a goal and works backward to determine the most efficient means of achieving it. This approach relies on prediction. If the future can be forecasted, then plans can be built with confidence. In environments with clear patterns and consistent data, this logic is highly effective.

Effectual reasoning takes a different approach. It starts from the available means: who I am, what I know, and whom I know, rather than from predetermined resources. These ingredients become the starting point for action. Rather than predicting the future, effectual thinkers engage with it. They experiment, observe what emerges, and adjust based on new information. This method is common among experienced entrepreneurs, though it is rarely named or taught in traditional leadership development.

The issue is not about choosing one logic over another. Both are valuable. The key is recognizing when each is appropriate. Effective leaders are those who can move between reasoning styles. They know how to plan when the path is clear and how to adapt when it is not. They apply disci- pline where structure is needed and improvisation where flexibility is essential.

But a third capacity often determines whether a leader can make that shift. It is the ability to translate across logics. To recognize not only what form of reasoning is needed, but to express it in a way others can understand, trust, and act on.

Translation allows leaders to bring people with them when moving between different modes of thinking. A leader who understands effectual reasoning may still fail if they cannot explain their logic to colleagues trained in causal models. Without translation, effectual action can appear erratic or risky. With it, those same actions can be understood as adaptive, strategic, and grounded in reality.

Translation is not just linguistic. It is cognitive and cultural. It involves listening to the assumptions others are making, discerning the logic behind their objections, and shaping communication in a way that resonates with their frame of reference. In effect, it turns internal fluency into shared understanding.

This capacity is particularly important in organizations with strong planning cultures. Leaders must learn to articulate emergence without sounding careless. They must demonstrate intent while navigating ambiguity. They must, at times, speak two languages at once, one rooted in control, the other in exploration.

It is worth noting that nearly every graduate business program teaches causal reasoning as the foundation of effective management. There are strong reasons for this. When environments are stable and past data is reliable, "causal logic" supports essential business functions such as forecasting, budgeting, scaling, and risk management.

What is often overlooked is that we begin life as effectual reasoners. As children, we learn by doing. We engage with our environment, adjust our behavior, and try again. Over time, formal education shifts us toward planning, control, and the search for certainty. We are taught to favor what can be measured. We begin to equate uncertainty with danger and intuition with risk.

Yet movement is often more valuable than certainty. Especially in moments of ambiguity, progress depends less on knowing the outcome and more on being willing to begin. Effectual reasoning offers a way to start without having everything figured out. It encourages leaders to use what they already have and take action in the presence of the unknown.

This is what gives multi-dimensional leadership its strength. It is not a rejection of structure. It is a broader approach to complexity. It recognizes that leadership requires both control and responsiveness, both clarity and experimentation. But also both fluency and translation. The missing link is not an add-on to existing models. It is a way of thinking that integrates what leaders already know with what the world increasingly demands.

This book is about making that link visible and usable. It is about helping leaders see what they may already be doing in parts and then deepening it into something they can use with intention and skill.

A LIFE LIVED:

Learning the Hard Way

When I first began teaching, I was fortunate. The university where I taught for the first ten years of my academic career had, in retrospect, a culture remarkably tolerant of "effectual behavior." I didn't call it that at the time, but looking back, I now understand that my way of working, thinking, and experimenting was not just accepted, it was encouraged.

I had a voice in the direction of the department. I played an active role in planning and served in several leadership roles, including faculty advisor for the entrepreneurship center. I was trusted, and I thrived.

So when I was hired by a new university to serve as the academic director of their entrepreneurship institute, I walked in feeling energized. The dean's office welcomed me with open arms. They told me how excited they were to have a "real entrepreneur" on board, someone who could bring students real-world experience, experimentation, and energy. I remember thinking, *This is going to be great. I get to be me.*

But it didn't unfold that way.

Almost immediately, the friction started. Nearly every week, I found myself in my supervisor's office, hearing some version of:

"We don't do things that way at our school."

"You're pursuing too many things. Pick one and work on it until you've reached your goal."

At first, I tried to adjust. I slowed down. I narrowed my focus. I tried to fit in. But eventually, I proposed a bold, high-profile program that I believed could elevate the institute's national reputation. The response was immediate and unforgettable.

"We're going to let you do this," my supervisor said, "but if you fail or embarrass us, I will fire you."

It was one of the most stressful periods of my professional life. I was under constant scrutiny. Every decision felt like a test. Even though the program became the most successful initiative the institute had ever run, my resignation was not only accepted, it was quickly and quietly welcomed.

For a long time, I was bitter. I felt misunderstood, unappreciated, and burned out. But eventually, I was able to reflect through the lens of the science I had come to know so well.

That's when I saw it clearly: the leadership around me wasn't hostile, they were causal. Intensely causal. They were operating from a model that valued planning, linear focus, and risk control.

In their eyes, any success that came out of my work had to be the result of their "management" of me and not my method. They simply couldn't see how an effectual approach could produce meaningful outcomes.

That insight changed everything.

I began to pay closer attention to institutional culture, viewing it less through the lens of personality and more through the lens of decision logic. I stopped interpreting resistance as opposition and started seeing it as a mismatch in reasoning.

Most importantly, I began learning how to translate. I stopped expecting others to understand my logic intuitively and instead started communicating my actions in language they could recognize.

That shift, from frustration to fluency, ultimately made me a better leader, teacher, and collaborator. And it's the shift I want to help others make, too.

PUTTING IT TO WORK: THREE DIMENSIONS OF APPLICATION

Industry

In rapidly shifting markets, most organizations rely on causal structures: formal hierarchies, long-range forecasts, and standardized strategic plans. These mechanisms are familiar, measurable, and often effective, especially in stable conditions.

But when the landscape shifts quickly, as it often does today, these structures can become brittle. The more unpredictable the environment, the less helpful prediction-based tools become.

This is where the value of effectual reasoning becomes clear. Organizations that integrate this approach into their leadership culture don't just become more nimble, they become more resilient. They support adaptive behavior as a valid strategy from the start, rather than treating it as a fallback when the plan fails. They make space for experimentation in the face of uncertainty, recognizing that some solutions emerge only through action and iteration.

But effectual reasoning alone isn't enough. For it to take root across a complex system, leaders must also be able to translate. That means making unfamiliar methods understandable to others, especially in departments or functions built on precision, control, or compliance. A product lead using effectual reasoning might iterate their way to a breakthrough, but without translation, their choices may look erratic to a finance team trained to expect stable forecasts.

Translation builds trust. It allows adaptive decisions to gain legitimacy in planning-driven cultures. When leaders can move fluently between reasoning styles and explain those movements, organizations can respond to change with both agility and coherence.

Professional Career

For individual professionals, especially those in mid- or senior-level roles, success often comes from mastering planning, execution, and control. These are rewarded behaviors. But when disruption hits, when a project derails, a market shifts, or a new role feels less defined, those same professionals may find themselves unprepared.

Multi-dimensional leaders don't abandon structure. They expand beyond it. They build fluency in both causal and effectual approaches. When a plan is possible, they make it. When the path is unclear, they act anyway, drawing on their means, relationships, and insight. They move forward with care and a willingness to learn through action, even when the path isn't fully clear.

This adaptability becomes visible over time. These individuals stay engaged during periods of ambiguity. They don't disappear in uncertainty; they lean in. Colleagues begin to see them as unusually resilient, less for never faltering, and more for how quickly they recover and navigate creatively.

But there's something else that makes them stand out: their ability to translate. They help others see the logic behind what they're doing. When they take a nontraditional step, they explain the reasoning in terms that align with their team's values and expectations.

In doing so, they bridge worldviews. They reduce the friction that often comes with new ideas. This makes them invaluable and more than executors; they become connectors, mentors, and change agents across boundaries.

Personal Life

In life outside of work, the same patterns hold. Many people wait for clarity before making a move, waiting for the "right time," the "perfect conditions," or for every unknown to be resolved. But life rarely offers those guarantees. Too often, that waiting becomes a source of inertia or regret.

Effectual reasoning offers a different way. It invites us to begin with what we already have: our skills, experiences, networks, and intuition. It encourages us to act with intention, grounded in responsiveness instead of impulse.To try something small, learn from the outcome, and adjust. This logic allows movement without perfect knowledge. It replaces the illusion of certainty with the practice of agency.

This reasoning can shape how we navigate relationships, health decisions, career changes, or creative pursuits. And just as in organizations, our personal choices often intersect with others' expectations. Family, friends, or partners may not always understand why we're making a particular choice. That's where translation becomes important.

Translation in personal life means articulating your reasoning in ways others can connect to. It's not just explaining what you're doing; it's helping others see how your choices are grounded, thoughtful, and aligned with shared values. This creates space for mutual understanding, even when paths diverge. It turns action into conversation.

In that sense, translation isn't just a leadership skill; it's a way of being with others in complexity. It allows us to live more intentionally in uncertain conditions, without becoming isolated in our decisions.

2

EFFECTUAL THINKING IN A CAUSAL WORLD

Most large organizations are built around one dominant approach to reasoning: the kind that begins with a clear goal and then moves through a process designed to reach it as efficiently as possible. This is often called causal reasoning, though it's not always named explicitly. It shows up in how plans are made, success is measured, and leadership is defined.

People in these systems are usually expected to predict what's coming. They're asked to make long-range plans, reduce uncertainty wherever they can, and deliver results that are easy to track and report. The assumption is that if you plan well and follow that plan with discipline, things will turn out the way they're supposed to.

In many cases, that assumption holds. Especially when the environment is relatively stable, and when past data really does help you make sense of what's coming next. In those settings, causal reasoning provides a kind of comfort. It brings order to complexity. It makes large-scale coordination possible. It helps people agree on what matters and how to work toward it.

This way of thinking doesn't just show up in operations. It's woven into the culture. Into how leadership is taught. Into how performance is evaluated. Into how authority is distributed and how progress is communicated. You see it in budget cycles, marketing plans, and product roadmaps. It's everywhere. And for a long time, it's been the backbone of how institutions function.

Causal reasoning helps organizations grow. It helps them allocate resources and allows them to promise something specific to stakeholders, and then show they've delivered on that promise. It creates structure and accountability. It makes things feel predictable, even when the systems themselves are large and complex.

That's part of why so many leadership development programs are built around it. MBA programs teach it. Strategic planning processes depend on it. And the people who move up in these organizations tend to be the ones who can operate well, inside this logic.

In many ways, it's the dominant language of leadership.

But then the environment starts to shift.

Sometimes gradually, sometimes suddenly, but in ways that make this approach feel less certain. The data doesn't tell the whole story anymore. Consumer behavior changes faster than the reports can track. Market conditions fluctuate. Technology evolves quickly. The cycles get shorter. The pressure to respond grows.

In those moments, the usual logic can start to feel too narrow. Technically correct, but less suited to the conditions.

In times of uncertainty, the future isn't just hard to predict; it may be fundamentally unknowable. When that's the case, a plan based entirely on past patterns may not be helpful. In fact, it might hold people back. It might delay the very actions that are needed.

That's when another way of thinking starts to matter more.

Effectual reasoning begins with a careful look at what's already available instead of what might be needed: who's here, what we know, what we're capable of doing right now.

Instead of asking, "How do we reach this goal?" the question becomes, "What can we do with what we have?"

And then it moves forward, slowly, iteratively, paying attention to what happens. Learning from real events rather than from projections. Revising based on what becomes clear in motion, rather than trying to nail everything down in advance.

This kind of thinking often looks different from the outside. It's less linear. It doesn't follow the same patterns. The steps aren't all laid out ahead of time. There's more adjusting. More noticing. More interaction with the environment, which can make it harder for systems grounded in causal logic to recognize what's happening or to trust it.

That's where the difficulty comes in.

It's not that organizations reject effectual thinking outright. Many of them talk about wanting innovation. They talk about agility or encouraging entrepreneurial behavior. They say they want people to take initiative, try new things, and move faster.

But then those same organizations evaluate those behaviors using causal standards. They want outcomes that can be forecast. They want experiments, but with predefined success metrics. They want risk-taking, as long as the risk is small and clearly bounded before anything begins.

They want something new, but only if it comes with guarantees.

For leaders who are trying to work effectually, that can be confusing. It can feel like being invited to explore and then penalized for not following the script. The behaviors that make innovation possible like pivoting, iterating, or acting before all the answers are known, may be seen as disorganized or reckless. Or worse, as evidence that the person leading the work doesn't have a clear strategy.

That can be hard to sit with, especially if the outcomes are positive, but the process doesn't look the way people expect it to.

This misalignment often has consequences for the people behind them.

Leaders who work this way may start to question their instincts. They may feel misunderstood or isolated. They may start to adjust how they present their work because it doesn't match what the organization is used to hearing, even if their approach is well grounded. Some learn to disguise what they're doing. Others eventually leave.

That's the tension this chapter is exploring.

Because there's another possibility, one that doesn't require abandoning the structure or hiding the instinct to explore.

It starts by recognizing that both ways of thinking have value. Different situations call for different tools. The work of leadership, now more than ever, involves knowing how to move between them.

Not for the sake of appearances. But because reality is rarely one thing or the other. And neither is the work.

THE DILEMMA: ADAPTIVE THINKERS IN RIGID STRUCTURES

Imagine being someone who tends to learn by doing. Someone who notices things as they emerge, who tests ideas early, and who believes that momentum often comes before clarity. That orientation, the willingness to move before all the answers are in, can feel intuitive. Natural, even. But it can also be difficult to explain, especially inside systems that expect a plan to come first and evidence to follow.

In many structured organizations, the dominant approach is to reward what looks familiar. Proposals are judged based on how clearly they align with existing goals. New ideas are expected to arrive fully formed, backed by data, with a clear path to execution. Change is accepted, but only if it fits inside a process. Deviations from the plan are viewed as something to correct, not as something that might hold value on their own.

For someone who works effectually, that setup can feel narrow because it doesn't leave much space for the kind of learning that happens through action, even when the logic is sound.

If you're someone who tends to move first and refine later, you might find that your work is hard to explain. Or that your choices are seen as impulsive. Or that what feels natural to you by pivoting when conditions change, following an emerging thread, testing something small instead of waiting for a perfect answer, is interpreted as a lack of discipline.

When that happens, you might hear familiar phrases. Phrases that aren't necessarily hostile, but still land with weight:

"You're moving too fast."

"We need a clearer plan before we act."

"That's not how we do things here."

These aren't just comments, they're signals. They tell you something about the system you're in. Usually, that system has been shaped to reduce uncertainty, not invite it.

For people who are wired toward effectual thinking, those signals can be hard to process because they often miss what's actually happening. What might feel like movement to one person feels like risk to another. What looks like responsiveness from the inside looks like unpredictability from the outside.

Over time, this disconnect can wear people down. They may begin to question their approach. They might feel pressure to conform or to hide the messier parts of their process.

In some cases, they'll try to fit in. In others, they'll start looking for a different place to work that allows more room to move.

What gets lost in the process isn't just the individual. It's the contribution they were trying to make.

These are often the same people who notice things early. They are comfortable taking a step forward before everything is certain. They act on weak signals, or see connections that others miss. And those instincts, the ones that don't always look polished, can be exactly what's needed when conditions are shifting.

CAUSAL VS. EFFECTUAL REASONING MATRIX

	Causal	Effectual
Starting Point	🎯 Set goal	Available means
Logic	⚙️ Prediction-driven	Exploration-driven
View of Uncertainty	⚠️ To avoid or minimize	To embrace and test
Action Style	✔️ Goal-oriented	Adaptive

Figure 2: This table highlights the fundamental differences between causal and effectual approaches to leadership. The comparison illustrates how each approach views uncertainty and action and why the ability to shift between them is essential for leading in dynamic environments.

CAUSAL VS. EFFECTUAL REASONING:
TWO LOGICS, ONE LEADER

This matrix offers a side-by-side view of two core reasoning styles that show up in leadership often without being named. While causal logic is the dominant framework in most organizational systems, effectual logic quietly drives much of the innovation, adaptation, and forward motion required in complex or shifting environments.

Understanding the difference matters. Causal reasoning begins with a goal and works backward. It thrives on predictability, control, and step-by-step execution. Effectual reasoning starts with what's available: your means, your relationships, your insight and builds forward, one move at a time. It embraces uncertainty not as a threat, but as a design condition.

Many leaders rely on one logic without realizing it. But multi-dimensional leadership asks something more: the ability to move between them. To recognize when the moment calls for a plan and when it calls for momentum. When control is useful, and when creativity is required. When to protect, and when to shape.

This visual isn't a ranking. It's a prompt. A mirror. A decision-making map.

Not every problem needs a strategy. Some need a starting point.

REFLECTION PROMPT

Think about a leadership challenge you recently faced, big or small.

- Did you begin with a defined outcome, or did you build from what you had?

- How did your approach to uncertainty shape your actions?

- Looking back, were you leading with causal logic, effectual logic, or some combination of both?

- What might have changed if you had shifted your logic midstream?

But they're not always recognized as strengths. Sometimes they're treated as liabilities. Or as quirks. Or as traits that need to be managed.

And that's part of the dilemma.

Effectual thinkers working inside rigid systems often find themselves stuck between their instincts and the expectations around them. They're told that innovation is welcome, but only if it arrives in a way that fits the process.

They're encouraged to be bold, but also to stay inside the frame. If they can't make their work legible in the language the system speaks, it may never gain traction because it doesn't look the way it's supposed to.

This is where translation becomes essential.

Not translation in the sense of pretending to be someone else, but in the sense of learning how to make the logic behind your actions visible to people working from a different frame. It's not about changing who you are. It's about finding a way to stay connected to what matters, while also helping others see the value of how you work.

That's a kind of leadership, too.

And for multi-dimensional leaders, it's often the part of the work that matters most.

FLUENCY OVER REBELLION: BECOMING MULTI-DIMENSIONAL

When people who think effectually run into resistance inside systems shaped by causal logic, their responses often drift toward the edges. Some pull back. They quiet themselves. They stop offering ideas that feel too different or too early.

Over time, they start to edit themselves because they're tired of being misunderstood, even though they haven't changed how they see things.

Others go the opposite direction. They push harder. They stop trying to explain. They move ahead without alignment, hoping the results will speak for themselves. They take risks quietly, or they disconnect from the structure altogether and start working around it out of frustration.

Neither approach tends to work for long. The people who withdraw often begin to feel small or stuck. Those who break away from risk become isolated or are seen as outsiders, even if their work is valuable.

But there is another way. It doesn't always show up right away, and it's not always easy to hold. Still, it offers a kind of possibility that the other responses don't.

I've come to think of it as the "path of the loyal rebel."

These are the leaders who aren't trying to overthrow the system. They're not dismissive of structure. In fact, many of them care deeply about the mission and want to see the organization thrive.

But they also recognize the limits of the system's default logic. They're willing to work at those edges to create space for something new without needing to prove a point.

They move effectually, but not in isolation. They stay in relationship with the system, even when it doesn't fully understand them. They speak up, not to provoke, but to serve. When they act in ways that don't match the norm, they take time to explain why. Plainly and without being defensive.

They don't pretend that the structure doesn't matter. They just understand that sometimes it needs to stretch.

This is the essence of multi-dimensional leadership.

People who lead this way don't discard one logic in favor of another. They learn to move between them. Sometimes they plan carefully. Sometimes they begin before they know where things will lead. They know how to run a process when the steps are clear and how to stay grounded when the path is still forming. They don't treat structure and improvisation as opposites. They treat them as parts of a broader toolkit.

Just as importantly, they learn how to communicate across those logics.

They don't just change how they act, they change how they explain.

They find ways to frame effectual behavior in language that feels familiar to causal systems, to build understanding without manipulating.

They talk about their experiments as pilots. They connect open-ended exploration to long-term goals. They describe early action as a way to learn something useful. They point to progress, even when the results are still emerging.

Over time, if they stay consistent, people begin to trust what they're doing because they've shown that they can hold uncertainty without losing direction, and without losing others along the way.

That ability to move fluidly across logics is rare. When it's done well, it often goes unnoticed, at least at first. It doesn't call attention to itself. It doesn't try to win arguments. It simply helps things move forward. Gently, steadily. With care.

In doing so, these leaders become something more than effective. They become bridges.

They hold the space between what is and what might be.

Between strategy and exploration.

Between the need for clarity and the need for movement.

It doesn't always feel like leadership, at least not in the usual sense. But it is. It's the kind that holds tension, listens as well as acts, and knows how to carry something through without needing to be the loudest voice in the room.

That kind of leadership can change more than just outcomes. It can change what's possible in the culture around it.

ANCHORING INSIGHT: INTEGRATION AS STRATEGIC LEADERSHIP

One of the shifts that often marks the difference between a competent manager and a more seasoned, adaptive leader is how they relate to the tools they've been given. It's not just about knowing how to use them. It's about knowing when they're needed and when they aren't.

Integration isn't about blending everything into one approach, it's about moving fluidly between different ways of thinking without getting stuck in one.

Most leaders are taught to rely on causal reasoning for good reason. When the goals are clear and the environment is relatively stable, it works. If you know where you're trying to go and the path to get there is reasonably visible, it makes sense to follow a structured plan. That kind of thinking keeps systems aligned. It helps with coordination. It reduces unnecessary risk.

But not everything fits into that frame. There are situations where the destination isn't clear yet. Or where the path is still forming. Or where what's needed isn't another plan, but a small move that makes learning possible.

In those moments, effectual thinking isn't just helpful. It becomes essential.

The leaders who seem to navigate those shifts well don't usually talk about it in grand terms. They seem to know when to plan and when to feel their way forward. They don't overidentify with one approach. They've seen enough situations to recognize that no single method works in every context. They trust themselves to choose based on the moment, not on a rule.

That kind of fluency, being able to work causally when things are stable and effectually when they're not, makes them flexible. But more than that, it's what makes them strategic. They're not just responding to what's in front of them, they're designing their approach based on what the moment actually calls for.

That's what often gets missed in conversations about innovation or transformation. We talk about vision, boldness, and change. But the real work, most of the time, is more grounded. It's about how decisions get made. What gets permission to move forward. How much space there is for learning that doesn't arrive fully packaged.

Most innovation initiatives are still built with causal language. Strategic plans. Milestones. Success metrics. But when you look closer, what's needed is something less predictable. New offerings. New partnerships. New ways of working. And those things tend to come through experimentation and revision, not through flawless execution of a fixed plan.

That's the paradox. Organizations ask for innovation, but often design it in ways that make it hard to deliver. They want fresh ideas, but want them vetted in advance. They want agility, but build systems that depend on consistency.

And this is where multi-dimensional leaders quietly do something different.

They don't try to force a change in culture overnight. They don't go to war with the system. Instead, they adjust how they work inside it. They shape their actions in ways that make room for uncertainty without making a show of it. They find language that keeps others with them. They create a little more space than was there before.

Over time, something starts to shift. People begin to notice that learning is happening. Progress is being made, even when the path isn't linear.

The structure doesn't break. It adapts. Not everywhere at once. But in the places where someone stayed present long enough to help it bend.

That kind of leadership doesn't always stand out. It doesn't need to. Its strength is in its steadiness. In its willingness to stay connected. In the way it earns trust, not just through results, but through the quality of its presence, especially when things are unclear.

The next chapter will offer a more structured way to think through this kind of decision-making. It's meant for the moments where certainty isn't available, and the work still needs to move forward. But before we turn to that, we'll stay here a little longer, with a story that brings these ideas into everyday life.

A LIFE LIVED:

Finding Our Way

I've been married for thirty-four years. My wife is sharp, deeply capable, and quietly formidable in the way she approaches work and life. We're both entrepreneurs, though we've gone about it in very different ways.

Over the years, we've each built our own businesses, and we've also built one together. There's been overlap, and there's been tension. And there's been a lot of learning.

If I were to describe her in terms of the ideas in this book, I'd say she operates from a strongly causal orientation. I mean that as a compliment. She plans carefully. She sets goals with intention. She works through problems in a structured, deliberate way. When she commits to something, she follows it through. She doesn't get pulled off course easily. That kind of steadiness has shaped a lot of her success.

I, on the other hand, lean much more toward effectual thinking. I move early. I tend to follow what's emerging. I adjust as I go. I'm comfortable starting without a clear outcome in mind because I often find that the best outcomes come from staying close to the work in motion. It's not reactive, and it's not improvisation for the sake of variety. It's just the way I naturally make sense of things.

Working together hasn't always been simple.

Early on, we hit points of friction even though our values were aligned because we approached problems so differently. She would want a clear plan before starting. I'd want to begin and figure things out along the way. She'd push for clarity. I'd resist the need to define everything too early. Neither of us was wrong, but we were often out of step.

What helped us, eventually, was realizing that our ways of working weren't in conflict. They were complementary. We had to learn how to see them that way.

That shift didn't happen overnight, and it didn't come from one conversation. It came from paying attention and noticing what each of us contributed beyond just what we preferred.

I began to see that she was the one who built stability into what we created. She was the one who could carry something through its growth phase with consistency and care. She didn't just start things, she sustained them. She protected what we had already built, even while I was looking for the next thing.

She came to see that my value wasn't just in energy or newness. It was in being able to see opportunities before they were obvious. To try something before it felt fully formed. To create momentum when things were still taking shape.

Eventually, we gave ourselves language for it. I became, in our shared story, the one who created opportunities. I was the one who looked outward, followed instinct, and brought things into motion. She became the steward of the business once it had form. The one who gave it rhythm, stability, and a structure it could grow within.

Once we understood that, the tension didn't disappear, but it changed. We started to trust each other's instincts more. We stepped into different roles more consciously. We began to see the working relationship as something that was stronger because of our differences.

My belief is that a team doesn't need perfect alignment to work well; it needs a mutual respect for how others make sense of the world.

What we found in our partnership is something I've seen again and again in organizations. The most resilient teams usually aren't the ones that all think the same way. They're the ones where different reasoning styles are understood, named, and given room to contribute.

People don't have to be convinced to think like each other, but they learn how to listen and work together even when they start from different places.

That kind of pairing: causal and effectual, isn't a compromise. It's often an advantage.

But only if it's made visible. And only if the people involved are willing to see the value in what they don't always understand right away.

PUTTING IT TO WORK: THREE DIMENSIONS OF APPLICATION

Industry

Most organizations don't have to choose between structure and adaptability. They often think they do, especially when change feels risky or when resources are tight. But the choice isn't between causal and effectual, it's in how the two are understood and used together.

That starts by noticing where "causal thinking" is doing more than it needs to. Sometimes planning cycles become so rigid that there's no room for ideas that haven't been fully modeled yet. Sometimes innovation efforts stall because the structure doesn't allow for early movement.

In those moments, a shift can begin by creating just a little more space. It might mean framing a new initiative as a useful experiment instead of a guaranteed outcome. It might mean making room for small bets that don't yet have proof behind them. Or naming learning as something that holds value on its own, even if it doesn't lead immediately to something measurable.

The shift doesn't have to be sweeping. Most of the time, it begins quietly. A pilot here. A reframing there. A leader who translates the logic behind an unorthodox choice in a way others can understand. Over time, these small moves, change how people relate to uncertainty and to each other.

Professional Career

If you tend to think effectually and you're working in a system that leans heavily on planning and control, it's easy to feel out of step. You might start to doubt your instincts or feel like you have to hide the way you work. But hiding often leads to disconnect. And over time, it can take a toll.

One way to stay connected to your way of thinking, without losing traction in the system around you, is through translation. Not performance. Just thoughtful, careful framing. You can talk about what you're doing in a way others can recognize.

That might mean presenting something uncertain as a low-risk pilot. Or showing how early movement ties into a larger strategic goal. Or identifying how the learning that comes from trying something will be useful, even if the outcome shifts.

If you're more naturally oriented toward causal thinking, you don't have to give that up. But it might help to notice what's missing when plans dominate every phase of the work. You might begin looking for small ways to act before everything is fully known. Or partnering with someone who thrives in ambiguity, and seeing what they notice that you don't. You don't need to become someone else, just be more spacious in how you move.

Either way, developing fluency in both logics gives you more range. That range can be quietly powerful, especially when the work gets messy.

Personal Life

These patterns don't just show up at work. You'll often find them in personal decisions, relationships, and even in how you travel or spend your free time.

Some people plan their vacations down to the hour. Others book a flight and figure it out when they get there. Some people wait until they're sure before making a move. Others try something small to see how it feels. Neither way is right. But noticing your default can help you see where you might be getting stuck and where you might need a different kind of movement.

In relationships, these differences can cause real tension. One person wants to decide and move forward. The other wants to explore and see what's possible. But if both people understand that these are simply different ways of reasoning, different ways of working with uncertainty, then the conversation can change. It becomes less about who's right and more about what's needed now.

In your internal life, it can be useful to ask whether you're waiting for certainty that may not come. Or whether you're holding back from something because the path isn't fully clear yet. Sometimes it's okay to move before you're sure. Sometimes that's where clarity comes from.

3

TRANSLATING ACROSS LOGICS

A lot of the breakdowns in leadership don't come from disagreement about what needs to be done. That's what we often assume, but in many cases, the tension isn't really about the task itself. It's about something more invisible. Something quieter.

What's often missing isn't the decision, but a shared understanding of why it's being made.

That gap doesn't always show up right away. It can sound like confusion, or feel like resistance, or look like misalignment. But underneath it, people are often thinking in very different ways, and they may not realize that the logic they're using isn't the same.

It's almost like they're speaking different languages without knowing it.

This happens more often than we tend to acknowledge. Most people don't name or explain their reasoning style. They assume it's understood.

In some environments, that assumption holds. But in more complex or diverse teams, especially when people are trained in different disciplines or come from different kinds of work, it can lead to friction that's hard to trace.

The truth is, the logic behind a decision is one of the most important and underappreciated aspects of leadership. Not just the outcome, or the plan, but the way someone makes sense of what they're doing. That logic shapes how ideas are evaluated. It shapes how risk is seen, how speed is interpreted, and how trust is built or lost.

And it's usually invisible until something doesn't land.

We often assume that if something makes sense to us, it will make sense to others. That our reasoning is shared. But it rarely is, especially when people are operating from different decision-making logics, like causal and effectual reasoning.

Causal logic has a structure that's widely understood. It starts with a goal, then maps a path toward that goal. You figure out the risks, make a plan, and execute it. It's straightforward, and it tends to translate well into spreadsheets and slides.

Effectual logic doesn't begin that way. It starts from a different place. It looks at what's available: what you already know, who's involved, what's possible right now, and moves forward from there. Instead of aiming at a fixed outcome, it adapts as it goes. It's not random, but from the outside, it can look a little loose. A little ambiguous.

Neither logic is better than the other. But they are different enough that, without some kind of translation, they can feel incompatible.

That's where many leaders start to stumble, and they stumble because the people around them can't see the logic behind the action. When that logic stays hidden, trust can slip away.

It's easy to assume that effectual thinkers are being erratic when what they're actually doing is adapting in real time. And it's just as easy to assume that causal thinkers are being inflexible when they may just be trying to bring order to a complex situation. Neither one is at fault. But without translation, both can feel at odds.

And so the friction begins.

If you lead with an effectual style, your approach might not make sense to others unless you take the time to explain it. If you're more naturally causal, you might find yourself frustrated when others act before there's a clear plan, especially if no one's talking about how that decision got made.

The skill that helps in both cases is the same: learning to translate and how to make your way of thinking visible in a way others can understand through connection as opposed to persuasion.

When leaders learn how to do this, it changes what's possible. Ideas move more easily. Teams start to align more naturally. What felt like tension becomes something that can be worked with.

In this chapter, we'll look at how translation works and what happens when it's missing. How to use it as a quiet, practical way of helping people move together by making it easier for others to follow.

Leadership isn't just about making decisions.

It's about making those decisions understandable enough that others can come with you.

THE COST OF MISUNDERSTANDING

Every organization has stories that don't make it into reports or strategy decks. Projects that didn't take off. Ideas that showed promise but slowly lost traction. Initiatives that were dropped, not because they were weak, but because something about them didn't quite land.

Often, what went wrong wasn't the idea itself. It was the way the idea was framed. Or maybe the way it wasn't.

When people don't explain the reasoning behind a decision, especially when it comes from a logic that's unfamiliar to others, things start to break down. Not loudly. Not all at once. But gradually. A little confusion here. A bit of hesitation there. Until, eventually, the work stalls.

You can see it happen in all kinds of places. A team proposes something new, but because it doesn't come with a forecast or a detailed plan, it gets flagged as too risky. Another team is learning fast, iterating on a prototype, trying to find a better fit . But, from the outside, it looks like they're just spinning. Another leader wants to wait for more clarity before moving, and people start to wonder if they're avoiding a decision altogether.

None of these behaviors is wrong. But without a clear explanation of what kind of logic is driving them, they can easily be misunderstood.

And once that misunderstanding sets in, it's hard to undo.

This is especially true in environments where different teams work from different mental models. Maybe the design team is working effectually, making changes in response to what they're seeing, and the finance team is working causally, trying to track forecasts and timelines.

When these teams meet, they're both doing good work. But they're using different logics. If no one names that difference, the conversation gets tense. Sometimes quietly. Sometimes not.

This happens more than we like to admit.

It wears people down. Relationships between departments become strained. Trust gets replaced with second-guessing. Leaders are judged not just for what they're doing, but for how well their actions match the expectations of the system around them.

When that match isn't there, it's easy to assume the problem is with the person.

That's one of the hardest things about this kind of misunderstanding. It doesn't show up as a problem with logic. It shows up as a problem with character. Someone seems reactive. Or overly cautious. Or not strategic enough. Once that label sticks, it's difficult to lead effectively, even if the work itself is sound.

Everyone sees Superman. Not everyone sees Clark Kent. But Lois Lane does. She knows who he really is, not just the costume, but the complexity underneath. And she never confuses performance for substance. She doesn't need to fly to matter. Her insight, her steadiness, her ability to hold the truth without needing to broadcast it, those things make the story work. It's a form of leadership that often goes unseen, but it's what allows others to lead, and few leaders know how to hold it.

Without Lois, Superman is only half the story.

This isn't about skill. It's about coherence.

People want to understand what others are doing and why. When they don't, they lose confidence in the person making the decisions.

When trust starts to erode, momentum often goes with it.

This is especially common in cross-functional environments, where different areas of the organization operate with different assumptions. One team is trying to learn in real time. Another is trying to manage risk. Both are doing what makes sense in their world. But when they come together, if they don't understand how the other is thinking, even small disagreements can start to feel like major misalignments.

Leaders, especially those trying to work across teams, often find themselves in the middle of that gap.

They're trying to support innovation, but also stay aligned with formal processes. They're encouraging exploration, but are also accountable for timelines and results. They want to move with care, but get told they're moving too slow. Or they try to move quickly and get told they're being reckless.

It's not that they're confused. It's that they're navigating two different systems of expectation and trying to stay credible in both.

That's the deeper cost of misunderstanding. It's not just missed opportunities. It's the slow erosion of trust in people who are doing their best to lead thoughtfully, but who aren't always being understood.

This is where translation becomes more than just helpful.

It becomes part of how leaders protect the integrity of their work by helping others see how it makes sense.

THE TENSIONS OF TRANSLATION

	Causal Thinker Sees...	Effectual Thinker Sees...
Speed	Recklessness	Rigidity
Status	Lack of respect	Control issues
Structure	Aversion to process	Guidance
Structure	Operational blindness	Boundaries

Figure 3: Common perception gaps between causal and effectual thinkers, highlighting the interpersonal friction that can occur when reasoning styles are misaligned

TRANSLATING ACROSS LOGICS:
WHERE MISUNDERSTANDING BEGINS

Leadership rarely fails because people don't care. It fails because people don't realize they're working from different mental models. One of the most invisible and costly sources of breakdown is a mismatch in reasoning logic.

Causal thinkers start with a defined goal and build backwards from it. Effectual thinkers begin with what's available and build forward. Neither approach is right or wrong. But without translation, their interaction often produces confusion, resistance, or conflict.

This map shows what that tension can look like in practice. It names the mismatch to surface what's really happening beneath the surface. These aren't personality clashes. They're logic clashes.

The work of leadership is to recognize the pattern early and translate across it. To give language to what the other side may not see. To slow the escalation of frustration and instead create clarity. Translation is not a compromise, it's a strategic behavior and it's one of the defining capabilities of a multi-dimensional leader.

REFLECTION PROMPT

Think back to a moment of conflict or misunderstanding in your work. Was it a disagreement about what to do or a disconnect in how people were thinking about the problem?

PSYCHOLOGY OF UNCERTAINTY: THE HIDDEN FORCE BEHIND RESISTANCE

There's something underneath all of this that's easy to overlook. Something that doesn't usually get talked about in meetings or planning sessions, but still shapes how people react, sometimes more than they realize.

It's the way uncertainty feels.

Not in the abstract, and not in theory. But in the body. In the nervous system. In that quiet, uneasy sense that something isn't settled, and might not be for a while.

There's research behind this. Neuroscience, psychology, behavioral studies. What they show is that uncertainty doesn't just make people uncomfortable. It activates stress responses. The brain interprets it as a kind of threat. The part of the brain that's involved in fear, what's known as the amygdala, lights up when we don't know what's coming. It's not that we're weak or unwilling to change, it's because that's how we're wired.

And that wiring shows up in how people work.

When things feel uncertain, many of us look for ways to reestablish control. We look for a path, a plan, or a framework that makes things feel organized again. That's part of why causal reasoning feels so reassuring. It offers structure. It gives us a way to move forward with a sense of clarity, even if that clarity is partial.

It's not just a management preference. It's a kind of emotional safety.

This helps explain why effectual behavior, when it isn't translated, can feel unsettling to some people. When someone moves without a clear outcome or shifts direction without explaining why, it doesn't just seem unfamiliar, it feels unsafe. Like the ground underneath is moving.

When that happens, the reaction can be stronger than the situation might seem to call for.

That doesn't mean the people reacting are being rigid. It means they're trying to stay grounded. They might not even realize it's about uncertainty. But what they're responding to isn't always the decision itself, it's the feeling of unpredictability that surrounds it.

This doesn't make causal thinkers wrong. It makes them human.

It gives us a reason to think differently about what translation is. It's more than just a way to explain yourself; it's a way to lower the sense of threat. To help people stay connected when the usual signals of safety, like plans, forecasts, and timelines, aren't fully available.

Effectual reasoning can still be structured. It can be thoughtful and deliberate and deeply grounded in logic. But that won't always be obvious to someone who's used to seeing those qualities in a different form.

Translation becomes a way to bridge that gap by helping others see how it's being held and how it's being worked with.

The leaders who do this well don't dismiss people's discomfort. They don't shame them for wanting clarity. They just offer another kind of clarity, one that comes from being transparent about the process instead of knowing everything in advance.

They don't ask people to be comfortable with ambiguity.

They help them feel safe enough to stay with it.

THE SKILL OF TRANSLATION

Once you start to see that uncertainty doesn't just cause confusion but actually creates stress, it becomes easier to understand why translation matters so much.

It's not a soft skill. It's not just about finding the right words or being persuasive. It's a way of helping people stay steady when things aren't clear. It's something you do to make the space more navigable for yourself and others.

When you're working across different kinds of reasoning, translation becomes part of how you lead.

Most people, even the most capable and experienced, don't always respond well to ambiguity, especially when they don't know how to read it. The brain is quick to fill in gaps when the logic behind something isn't visible. And those guesses often lean toward doubt or discomfort, not trust.

That's part of what makes working effectually hard to understand from the outside. If you're adjusting as you go, or responding to what's emerging, and no one knows why you're doing it that way, it can seem like there's no structure at all. Even if you're thinking carefully. Even if there's a clear method underneath.

Translation helps make that structure visible by showing that there's logic in the movement. That there's something deliberate happening, even if it doesn't follow the usual format.

It helps reduce the mental strain for others, too.

When people are asked to engage with something unfamiliar, their brains tend to work harder. They use more cognitive effort to make sense of what they're seeing.

When that effort gets too high, when things feel too confusing or too ambiguous, it becomes harder to focus. People fall back on habits. They stick with what they already know, and they may reject something because it feels too far outside their frame.

That's why even good ideas or useful actions can be resisted when they aren't translated. It's not always about the content. It's about the effort it takes to understand it.

So when you offer people something they can hold onto: a familiar term, a clear frame, a visual anchor, you give their mind a way to stay engaged. You help them see the logic in something they might not otherwise recognize. That makes it easier to trust what's happening, even if it's unfamiliar.

This is what translation does. It lowers the pressure. It turns something that feels vague into something that can be followed because you've made it feel less threatening.

That's why fluency and translation are not the same.

Fluency is what gives you range and it's what lets you move between different ways of thinking without getting lost.

Translation is what gives you reach. It's what lets others come with you.

A lot of leadership work lives in that difference.

The people who can do both, who can think flexibly and also make that thinking accessible, often become the ones others turn to when things get complicated because they know how to move forward without leaving people behind.

HOW TO TRANSLATE TO EFFECTUAL REASONING TO CAUSAL AUDIENCES

If you tend to work effectually, meaning you start with what's available, move in small steps, and adjust as you go, you've probably had moments where that way of working has felt hard to explain.

Especially in systems that expect plans.

It's not that your thinking isn't sound. It's just that it doesn't always come with the kind of framing that people are used to seeing. And when that framing is missing, it's easy for others to feel uncertain. Or uneasy. Even when what you're doing is careful and thoughtful.

That's where translation becomes part of the work.

It's not about dressing up your thinking to make it look more formal. It's about helping people recognize that there's structure, even if it's not the kind they usually expect. You're not changing how you work. You're just taking the time to explain it in a way that makes others feel steadier.

There are a few ways to do this. None of them is complicated, but they do require some attention.

You might start by framing your early steps as structured discovery. Words like "pilot" or "prototype" can be helpful because they give people something familiar to hold onto. You're saying, "This is an experiment, but it's a focused one." It has boundaries. It's not just wandering.

It also helps to make progress visible. When your work is evolving in response to what you're learning, it can feel like things are shifting too much or too fast. Offering something concrete like a short-term deliverable, a visible learning outcome, even a simple summary of what's changed and why, can give people a sense of continuity. They don't have to wonder whether anything's happening. They can see it.

It's also important to name what's unknown. That might sound risky, but for many people, it builds trust. When you say, clearly and calmly, "Here's what we don't know yet, and here's how we're paying attention to it," it helps others relax. They don't have to guess whether you've considered the risks. They know you have.

Even though effectual reasoning often relies on informal cues and emergent insight, you can still build in regular check-ins. These don't have to be rigid. They're just touchpoints, moments to reflect, to share updates, to give others a way to stay connected to what's happening. That alone can go a long way.

None of these things requires you to stop working the way you work. What they do is make the logic more legible. They help others feel oriented, which makes it easier for them to trust what's unfolding even if they wouldn't have started there themselves.

The same holds in the other direction.

If you tend to work causally, starting with a goal and building a plan, and you're leading people who think more effectually, there's a kind of translation needed there, too.

You don't have to give up your structure, but it can help to loosen it slightly, without losing clarity. That might mean offering direction without prescribing steps, or naming what success might look like, while leaving room for people to find their way toward it.

Sometimes what's needed is just a shift in tone. Instead of saying, "This is the plan," you might say, "Here's what matters most. Let's see how we get there."

While it's important to give people space to explore, it's also okay to hold certain boundaries. You can create room for emergence without removing the edges entirely. That can actually support creativity, because it offers a sense of safety. People know what they're working within.

In both directions, what matters is the same.

You're not trying to change someone else's logic. You're trying to make your own easier to follow. That often means being a little more explicit. A little more patient and a little more willing to show your work because it makes things feel more navigable instead of feeling the need to defend it.

In most systems, that's what helps things move.

Not just better ideas. But clearer ways of sharing them.

ANCHORING INSIGHT: TRANSLATION AS STRATEGIC CREDIBILITY

Translation isn't just about being understood. And it's not only about helping others feel comfortable with the way you work. It's also part of how leaders build credibility, especially in systems that rely on alignment and shared understanding to function.

In most organizations, decisions don't stand on their own. They need to make sense to the people around them. Over time, that sense-making becomes a kind of currency. It's what builds or erodes trust.

This doesn't mean you have to justify every move. It does mean that if others can't follow your logic, if they don't understand how you got from point A to point B, they're less likely to support the work. Or to repeat it. Or to defend it when it gets questioned.

That's why translation isn't just a communication skill. It becomes part of how leadership works at a strategic level.

It's not just about decisions that go well. There's research showing that people are more likely to trust leaders who explain their thinking, even when the outcome is uncertain, than leaders who stay quiet, even if their decisions are technically correct. In one study, it turned out that what built credibility wasn't accuracy, it was coherence.

That's a useful thing to keep in mind. In complex environments, certainty is rare, and outcomes are often delayed. But the ability to narrate your reasoning in a way others can follow? That builds trust in the moment, not just in hindsight.

Part of the reason this works has to do with how people respond to ambiguity. When reasoning is unclear, the brain tends to treat that lack of clarity as a potential threat. It starts to scan for risk. It becomes more cautious and more critical. It begins to doubt the idea as well as the person behind it.

Translation gives people something steady to hold onto. A thread they can follow. A shape they can recognize. Even if the work is still unfolding.

In formal systems, especially those that are more structured or analytical, this matters a lot. It's not enough for your decisions to feel right to you. Others need to be able to explain them, too. They need to be able to talk about them in meetings, reflect them in reports, or defend them in front of stakeholders. They can't do that if they don't understand the logic.

That's one of the reasons effectual thinking can get overlooked, even when it's working. If it doesn't translate well into the formats others expect: slides, budgets, talking points, it might not get traction. Or recognition. Or support.

But when it does translate, everything changes.

That's why people who can speak both languages, who can hold ambiguity and still offer clarity, often find themselves in positions of quiet influence. They aren't louder than everyone else, but they're often easier to trust because they know how to carry it in ways others can follow.

And the systems around them respond to that.

Sometimes slowly. But they do.

Because even structured organizations, the ones that resist ambiguity the most, tend to reward the people who can explain it.

It's a quiet kind of leadership. One that doesn't depend on charisma or polish. It depends on being able to say, "Here's why this makes sense," in a way that others can repeat. That kind of coherence doesn't remove the uncertainty, but it makes the uncertainty feel navigable.

In environments where people are already stretched, where trust, time, and attention are all in short supply, that can make a real difference.

A LIFE LIVED:

Learning to Speak Their Language

Over the years I've worked at my current institution, there have been three major leadership transitions. Each one brought new people, new priorities, and a slightly different sense of what mattered most. That kind of change isn't unusual, but it has a way of making things feel less certain especially when you're trying to build something long-term.

Each time a new leader arrived, I found myself needing to reintroduce my work and the thinking behind it. For a while, that didn't go especially well.

I would bring forward an idea, something I had been developing for a while. I'd thought it through, tested parts of it, and felt confident it could make a real impact. These weren't loose concepts. They were grounded, and I believed in them.

But the responses I got were often cool. Not hostile. Just cautious. A lot of hesitation. Some ideas went nowhere. Others took months to gain even minimal traction.

At first, I took it personally. I wondered what I was missing. I didn't think I was being unclear. I wasn't rushing. But something wasn't connecting.

It took me a while to see it. But when I began to understand the difference between causal and effectual reasoning, something clicked.

I realized I had been working and communicating through an effectual lens. I was leading with what I had, following relationships and momentum, shaping things through interaction and adjustment. I hadn't been explaining that. I was just doing it, assuming the logic would be clear.

But these new leaders were coming from a different place. Their orientation was more causal. They expected to see a clear goal, followed by a structured plan. They wanted to understand the risks, the timeline, the expected return. If that wasn't front and center, they weren't sure how to engage.

They weren't ignoring my ideas. They just didn't know how to read them.

Once I understood that, I didn't change what I was doing. But I did start presenting it differently.

I began sharing more context: who I was meeting with, what I was noticing, where the energy was coming from. Not in a performative way. Just to show that things were moving. That I was paying attention. That nothing was happening in the dark.

I also started framing my proposals in ways that matched how these leaders made decisions. I organized the material differently. I led with goals. I talked about alignment. I named the risks and then walked through how they were being managed.

I treated conversations less like informal updates and more like qualitative data. I started tracking patterns in the feedback I was hearing. I paid closer attention to language: what people responded to, what made them hesitate, what helped them relax.

Where possible, I translated insights into something more tangible. A dashboard. A simple framework. A set of metrics that could stand alongside the story. Even when the work was still evolving, I gave it a form that others could work with.

None of this changed the heart of what I was doing.

But it changed how I was seen.

And that changed everything else.

Ideas started to move more easily. The questions I got were more constructive. The conversations shifted from skepticism to curiosity. I began to feel that the people around me weren't just tolerating my work, they were starting to trust it.

Not because the ideas themselves were different, but because the logic behind them had become easier to follow.

PUTTING IT TO WORK: THREE DIMENSIONS OF APPLICATION

Industry

In most structured environments, translation isn't just helpful, it's often what makes it possible for new ideas to stay alive long enough to take root. Especially in systems that depend on clarity, predictability, and consensus, the way something is framed often matters just as much as what it is.

Organizations that want to encourage innovation or adaptive thinking usually have to make space for different ways of reasoning. That space doesn't create itself. It has to be shaped.

One way to begin is by giving people shared language. That might mean naming the difference between causal and effectual thinking, and helping people see both as valid. It might mean adjusting how projects are presented to make the reasoning easier to follow without changing the substance.

Some teams build translation directly into their internal tools. A proposal template might include a section on "logic of approach." A planning document might offer room to note where learning is still happening. A check-in might be framed around insight instead of just milestones.

In some organizations, translation is practiced more informally. A leader pauses to explain why a shift is happening. A team member takes a moment to reframe a fast-moving project in language a cautious stakeholder can receive. These small moments make the system more breathable. They lower the friction. They help people stay with things that don't follow the usual path.

Over time, those moments add up. What once felt unfamiliar starts to feel more natural because more people have learned how to make their logic visible in ways others can trust.

Professional Career

Wherever you are in your work, whether you're leading a team, managing a project, or trying to make sense of a shifting role, your ability to explain how you think can quietly shape how others see you.

You don't have to narrate everything. But when the path you're taking isn't the one others might expect, a little translation can make a big difference. It can help others stay connected to the work and you.

If you lead effectually, it might help to be more deliberate in how you describe your process. You don't need to add formality where it doesn't belong, just enough shape to show that you're not improvising without care. You're responding. You're learning. You're moving with intention.

If you're more grounded in causal thinking, it might help to slow down your judgments when someone else works differently. Instead of asking why they aren't following the plan, you might ask what they're learning. What's shifting. What's emerging. That doesn't mean letting go of structure. It means letting in other ways of making sense.

Whatever your default, the more you can move between these logics and help others move with you, the more range you have. That range doesn't just help with decision-making. It helps with trust. With collaboration. With the day-to-day work of being in complex systems with other people who think in different ways.

Personal Life

This isn't just about work.

These patterns, how we make decisions, how we explain ourselves, how we respond to uncertainty, show up everywhere. In partnerships. In friendships. In families. Sometimes even more strongly than in professional settings, because they feel personal.

You may find that in your closest relationships, the conflict isn't really about the decision at hand. It's about how that decision was made. Whether someone felt included. Whether the logic felt shared.

In those moments, translation can be an act of care.

Not to get agreement. Not to win. Just to say, "Here's how I was thinking about it." Or, "Here's what felt true to me at the time." That doesn't solve everything. But it opens the door. And often, that's enough.

You don't have to abandon your way of thinking. You just have to be willing to show it.

And to listen when someone else does the same.

4

SENSE-MAKING AS A LEADERSHIP PRACTICE

HOW LEADERS CREATE DIRECTION WITHOUT NEEDING CERTAINTY

There are times when leadership feels less like deciding and more like trying to name what's happening because what's in front of you is still taking shape, rather than because you're unsure of your role, or afraid to move.

You're not the only one feeling it; the team is sensing it too. The system is quieter than usual in some places and more volatile in others. Things are moving, but it's not yet clear which way they're moving or what might come next.

This is not the kind of moment most leaders are trained for, especially in organizations where movement is expected to follow direction, not the other way around. In those places, there's often an unspoken rule that the leader should speak first. Should name the goal. Should lay out the plan and then tell others how to follow it.

That way of leading still works in certain situations. It works when the pattern is familiar. When the path is known. When the work ahead is more about execution than interpretation.

But not everything works that way, and not every system is stable enough to allow it.

Sometimes you're in a moment that doesn't match what came before. The data might be thin. The signals might be conflicting. The pressure might be rising, but the picture still hasn't settled. Even if you've seen something like this before, it doesn't feel the same. The edges are softer. The ground doesn't quite hold.

In those moments, people still look to the leader, but not necessarily for a decision. They're listening for something more subtle. They're trying to figure out how to interpret what's happening. What to make of the signals. What kind of posture they should take. Whether to move or wait. Whether the unease they're feeling is something shared or something they're carrying alone.

The only person who can help with that is the person holding the frame. The one whose voice still carries some weight. Who others assume can see a little farther or feel the contours of the moment more clearly. That doesn't mean you have to know the answer. It just means you're the one people are watching to figure out how to understand what's going on.

That's the part of leadership that often goes unnamed. The part that doesn't come with a playbook. It's not a decision or a declaration. It's more like sense-making. You're not trying to explain everything. You're trying to help others see more clearly what's already there. And to do that without rushing it. Without forcing it into a shape it's not ready to take.

This doesn't mean giving up control. What it asks for is a different kind of control. The kind that comes from being grounded. The kind that comes from knowing how to stay present when the picture isn't finished. The kind that helps others move because enough is visible to begin, in spite of the perceived uncertainty.

THE STRATEGIC ROLE OF MEANING

People don't just follow instructions. They follow meaning. They follow tone. They follow whatever feels real enough to hold onto. Sometimes that's a plan, if the plan still makes sense.

But other times, it's not the plan at all. It's the pauses. It's the small, offhand signals. It's the way a leader interprets what's happening in a way that doesn't flatten it or rush past it. It's something that feels like orientation, even if it's incomplete.

That kind of meaning is hard to manufacture, and it's almost impossible to fake. It comes from being willing to stay close to what's real, even when what's real doesn't lend itself to easy answers. It requires a kind of steadiness and not certainty, exactly, but a willingness to hold the ambiguity without letting it spill into chaos.

Research suggests that people perform better, stay more engaged, and are more likely to collaborate effectively when they believe the work has meaning, even when that meaning isn't fully defined. It doesn't need to be heroic or world-changing; it just needs to feel coherent. Something that can be lived with. Something that connects what they're doing today to something that still matters tomorrow.

That sense of coherence, especially in complex or fast-changing environments, has been shown to reduce anxiety and increase adaptive behavior. It helps people regulate themselves when the system around them is unsettled.

But organizations don't always create room for that kind of meaning to emerge. There's often pressure, both formal and informal, to provide answers as quickly as possible. Leaders are expected to step in and clarify things. Even when the clarity isn't there yet. Especially when the clarity isn't there yet.

That pressure doesn't just come from others; it comes from inside too. Especially for leaders who are used to being the one who steadies the room by saying something definite, who have earned trust through decisiveness, or who feel responsible for keeping others from feeling lost.

But in uncertain systems, clarity doesn't always come on command. Meaning doesn't always present itself right away. Sometimes it arrives sideways, and sometimes it unfolds through conversation, observation, or something that only starts to make sense after it's been sitting with you for a while. Sometimes the meaning only becomes visible after people start moving. It doesn't precede the action, it gets built alongside it.

That's why this part of leadership matters. When people don't understand what they're seeing, or when the framing keeps changing, they don't just lose focus, they start filling in the blanks themselves, and what they fill it with depends on what they're carrying.

Some might fill it with fear, and others with past experiences. Yet others fill it with assumptions about what's expected. That's how drift begins, because they're trying to anchor themselves, and no one is helping them do that well.

This is the work; helping others stay oriented while they're still inside the uncertainty. Naming what's unfolding, not perfectly, not completely, but honestly, by offering a shape to the moment without pretending it's fixed.

That's what sense-making is. It's not about knowing more than others. It's about being willing to say what you see. To help others hold the same questions. To say, "Here's what we know so far, here is what we're paying attention to, here's what we're wondering about together."

That kind of language doesn't end the ambiguity. But it gives people something to walk with. It gives them a way to stay in the work without feeling like they're on their own, and it reminds them that the uncertainty isn't something they're supposed to solve alone. It's something the team is holding together.

When people feel that, they stay more connected. They don't need to retreat into avoidance or overcontrol. They stay curious longer and share more. They become more thoughtful about the risks they take because they've been invited into a shared understanding of what's happening. That understanding, partial as it may be, is what gives motion its direction.

That's not a soft skill, nor is it window dressing; it's part of the actual structure of forward momentum. Meaning isn't a layer we add after the plans are made; it's one of the things that helps people know which plans are even worth making.

HOW LEADERS BUILD CLARITY WITHOUT OVERREACH

There's a kind of pressure that shows up in uncertainty and doesn't always announce itself. Sometimes it just hums in the background. It comes from the part of us that wants to steady the room. The part that believes leadership means offering direction, and sometimes it does, but not always. Not in every moment.

Sometimes what people need most is not a direction, but a way to understand where they are. Not a plan, but a frame. Something that helps them recognize the shape of what's unfolding, even if they can't yet see where it leads.

This is hard to do when you've been trained to lead through structure. When the systems around you still reward clarity over presence. When you've internalized the idea that a good leader always has the next step ready, even if the next step doesn't exist yet. Even if it's still becoming.

So what do you do instead? How do you offer clarity without pretending to know more than you do?

One way is to frame the moment, not the outcome. That means giving people language for what's happening now, without rushing into what it's supposed to become. It means saying things like, "Here's what seems to be shifting," or "This is the part we're starting to understand." That kind of framing doesn't lock anything in place, but it keeps people from spinning out. It gives them a way to track what's changing, and what hasn't yet taken form.

Another way is to resist the urge to oversimplify. When people are uncomfortable, there's a natural pull toward explanation. Toward making things neat. But systems in motion are rarely neat. And simplification can become a kind of erasure. So instead of collapsing the complexity, you can choose to carry it. Not all of it at once, but enough to keep the picture honest.

This takes patience. It takes language that doesn't overpromise and a willingness to sit with partial answers publicly instead of privately. To be the one who says, "This part is still emerging." or "We're watching this closely, but it hasn't settled yet."

Sometimes clarity is not about explaining something. It's about naming what's not yet explainable and doing that with enough steadiness that others don't mistake it for drift.

You can also create clarity by naming what people *can* do in the meantime. Even small steps help. Especially when those steps are connected to what's already visible. You're not giving them a solution, you're helping them stay inside the work.

That might mean collecting more input or it might mean staying in conversation. It might mean looking at the same data with fresh eyes. These aren't dramatic moves, but they're anchoring ones.

This kind of leadership is quiet and can be hard to see if you're looking for decisiveness in the usual way. But it's a kind of strength and it's the kind that helps teams hold their shape when things around them are still in flux. It's the kind that doesn't rush toward certainty just to make the discomfort stop. It stays long enough to ensure the frame is real.

When people feel that frame as something shared, they're more likely to stay engaged. More likely to bring their full attention. More likely to move in ways that keep the system open, rather than narrowing it too soon.

That's a kind of clarity, too, the kind that keeps people from getting lost without trying to fix everything.

THREE BEHAVIORS OF INTERPRETIVE CONTROL

This kind of leadership can be difficult to describe because it doesn't always look like leadership in the way most people expect. It's not decisive in the classic sense. It's not built on confidence or control in the way those words usually get used, but it's not passive either. It's not waiting around for things to become clear. It's an active kind of attention. It's a form of forward movement that works through interpretation rather than instruction.

I've noticed that while their words and actions may differ, the instincts of leaders who are good at this are remarkably similar. Those instincts show up in how they carry themselves when things are uncertain by staying close to the situation and helping others stay close too.

Here are three behaviors that I've seen hold up across different settings as *habits of presence*, as opposed to techniques.

They acknowledge what's known and what's not.

This might sound obvious. But it's rare to hear someone do it in a way that feels grounded. Most of us are trained to present what we know with confidence and keep the rest quiet. Or to say, "We don't know yet," in a way that signals distance, dismissal, or frustration. But that doesn't help. It usually just adds to the sense that something's wrong.

Multi-dimensional leaders who are practiced in sense-making don't avoid the gaps. They name them in plain language. They say things like, "Here's what we're sure of," and "Here's what still feels unsettled." They speak without needing to resolve everything. By doing that, they help others hold the ambiguity without feeling like it's theirs alone to carry.

They speak in arcs, not absolutes.

There's a rhythm to how these leaders talk. They don't make abrupt turns. They don't drop in conclusions that feel disconnected from what's still unfolding. They speak with a sense of trajectory. They stay close to the moment, but they also give people a sense of direction, something to look for, something to notice, something to feel alongside the facts.

They might say, "We're still in the early stages of this," or "What we're seeing so far is starting to tell us something, but we're not at the end of the story." That kind of language helps people move without locking them into a specific route. It creates space for things to shift. It lets people feel like they're part of a process, rather than waiting on a verdict.

They help others build the logic of the now.

THE INTERPRETIVE LEADERSHIP MAP

	Directive Management (Naming What's Known and Moving with It)	**Interpretive Leadership** (Staying Close to What's Real)
Stable / Predictable ↑ **Unstable / Unfolding ↓**	• The environment is familiar enough to move • Clarity is available and appropriate • Leadership offers structure without overreach	• The picture is still unfolding, but presence is steady • Framing the moment, not forcing resolution • Trust is built through honest ambiguity
	Overreach & Drift (Hesitating When Clarity Is Possible)	**Premature Certainty** (Certainty That Can't Hold)
	• The system is stable, but the leader holds back • Language stays soft when it could be grounding • Others begin to drift without needing to	• Signals are still in motion, but the leader declares a path • Pressure to perform clarity overrides what's actually known • Confidence gets mistaken for control—but it's brittle

Figure 4: *A comparison of how causal and effectual logics shape opportunity development.*

THE INTERPRETIVE LEADERSHIP MAP: UNDERSTANDING HOW LEADERS NAVIGATE AMBIGUITY WITHOUT OVERREACH

Leadership isn't always about having the answer; it's about knowing how to stay present when the answer is still forming. This map offers a way to understand four leadership behaviors that emerge in different combinations of clarity and system stability.

When environments are relatively stable and familiar, leaders can draw on **Directive Management** to name what's known and move the team forward with structure. But when things begin to shift, when signals are weak, tensions surface, or clarity fades, another kind of leadership is needed.

Interpretive Leadership is the practice of staying close to what's real, even when the picture is incomplete. These leaders resist the pressure to perform false clarity and instead frame the moment honestly. They build trust not by controlling the narrative, but by guiding others through honest ambiguity.

The other two quadrants reveal common traps. **Overreach & Drift** happens when leaders hesitate in moments that call for clarity, causing confusion and fragmentation. **Premature Certainty** occurs when leaders force resolution too soon—often mistaking confidence for control even though the situation is still unfolding beneath the surface.

The most effective leaders don't just toggle between clarity and ambiguity— they hold both with discipline and presence. They know when to ground a team and when to hold space for what's still emerging.

REFLECTION PROMPT

Think about a moment when the system around you was in motion; something was shifting, but it wasn't fully clear yet.

- How did you respond?
- Did you find yourself trying to create certainty or leaning into the ambiguity?
- Were you offering structure, or holding space?
- What did your team need most in that moment—and what did they receive from you?

What quadrant of the map did you occupy and how might your leadership have shifted if you had chosen a different stance?

This is the behavior that often gets overlooked because it doesn't show up as a bold move. It shows up in how leaders help others interpret their own experience. They might ask, "What are you noticing?" or, "What feels different this week than last?" They might reflect something back that's been said quietly, or show how two disconnected threads are actually part of the same shift.

It's not about being the one with the answer. It's about helping others find the throughline in what's already happening. That's how people start to reengage with the present moment, because they've had a chance to reconnect with what they already know.

When that happens, movement starts to feel possible again because people are no longer waiting for someone to resolve the uncertainty for them. They've been given enough to act and to stay with it while the rest continues to unfold.

BARRIERS TO LEADING THE WAY

Most leaders don't resist sense-making because they don't know how to do it. The problem isn't capability. It's context and what the system around them reinforces. The way certain behaviors get rewarded and the way others get quietly dismissed, misunderstood, or ignored.

In most organizations, especially ones with strong planning cultures, there's still an underlying belief that leadership means knowing. That it means having an answer and presenting it in a way that feels confident and complete. When a leader pauses, names uncertainty, or reflects what's still emerging rather than declaring what's decided, it can cause discomfort. Sometimes subtle, but sometimes not.

That discomfort often doesn't come from malice or resistance. It comes from expectation. From years of socialization inside systems that treat ambiguity as something to minimize or fix.

In those systems, clarity becomes a currency and certainty becomes a stand-in for control. Even when leaders know that the situation is still unfolding, they feel pressure to shape it into something firmer than it really is.

This is especially true in cultures where leadership is tightly linked to performance. Performance that's measured against forecasts and goals that were set before the conditions changed. Research on organizational behavior suggests that leaders in these systems face what's often called "signal distortion," the quiet, persistent tendency to filter or edit what's visible to protect alignment with the plan. It's not always intentional. But it's real. And over time, it weakens both trust and responsiveness.

There's also the challenge of visibility. Sense-making isn't always visible in the same way execution is. You can point to an initiative. You can show a plan. You can track outputs. But sense-making is relational. It's cumulative. It happens through conversations, reflections, and framing choices that don't always get captured in reports or dashboards. It can look like the leader isn't doing enough, isn't moving fast enough, or isn't sure what they're doing at all.

In performance systems that privilege tempo, that can create friction. The quiet kind that builds slowly. Leaders who are trying to hold uncertainty well, who are pacing their language carefully, who are working to understand what's really shifting before they respond, can start to feel like they're falling behind. Even if they're the ones seeing most clearly.

That pressure isn't just external. It gets internalized. Especially by leaders who care. The ones who don't want to mislead people. The ones who know how fragile trust can be. The ones who've learned, sometimes the hard way, that it's better to say less than to overpromise.

Those leaders often end up walking a fine line. They hold back when they should speak, or they speak before they're ready. Sometimes they try to do both by offering partial truths with too much polish, which only creates more confusion later.

There's also the problem of language. Words like "clarity" and "alignment" and "communication" are used everywhere but they don't always mean the same thing. One person's clarity is another person's oversimplification. One person's alignment is another person's control.

When those definitions aren't shared, leaders who are trying to do the real work of sense-making can start to feel like they're speaking a different language. The very thing they're trying to offer, grounded presence and careful framing, is being misread as uncertainty or indecision.

It doesn't take long for that to wear on people. Not always in dramatic ways, but in quiet ones. Over time, they start to edit themselves. They stop naming what feels off. They present their thinking in ways that are easier to digest. They protect the system from the discomfort it needs to feel because they've learned how quickly discomfort gets confused with failure.

When that happens, something subtle but important gets lost. Not just a piece of information. Not just a helpful insight. What gets lost is the opportunity to understand what's really happening. What gets lost is the chance to stay connected to what's unfolding before it's been forced into a shape.

Because when leaders pull back like that, others follow. People start relying on surface cues. They stop offering interpretations of their own. They wait for direction that never quite comes, or they begin to create meaning in isolation. Based on experience. Based on fear. Based on whatever feels safest to believe.

The risk isn't that the system slows down, but that it starts to fragment, and people move from shared meaning to private explanation. Trust gives way to guessing, and momentum is replaced with drift.

These are the costs that don't always show up on a dashboard. But they're real. And they're cumulative. They often begin when leaders are discouraged from doing the very thing that helps others stay present, which is noticing what's real and being willing to say so. Even when it's unfinished.

HOW INTERPRETIVE LEADERS BUILD TRUST

Trust doesn't always come from having the answer. More often, it comes from knowing that someone is paying attention. They're staying close to what's happening. They haven't stepped out of the moment to wait for the story to settle.

It comes from a presence that's more than physical, it's one that's cognitive and emotional as well. The kind that shows up in how someone speaks, how they listen, and how they hold uncertainty in front of others without letting it overwhelm the room.

This kind of presence creates a different kind of trust. It's not built on authority or charisma. It's not about being the one with the clearest vision. It's about being the one who doesn't flinch when things are still unclear. The one who doesn't rush to explain it all away. The one who holds the tension without making it heavier for everyone else.

There's a fair amount of research behind this. Studies on trust formation suggest that consistency, transparency, and shared sense-making matter more in volatile environments than formal expertise or positional power. Some of the most compelling work focuses on behavioral integrity, the perceived alignment between what leaders say and what they actually do.

When that alignment holds, especially under pressure, trust tends to deepen. But when there's even a small gap between words and behavior, trust begins to erode quickly and often quietly.

In those moments, the mismatch doesn't need to be dramatic. It might be as simple as a leader speaking with too much certainty when the team knows the situation is still shifting or promising a level of clarity that the work can't yet support.

What people feel isn't just confusion, it's a kind of distance. They begin to question whether what's being said still reflects what's real, and once that questioning starts, it becomes harder to know what to follow.

Simons' research shows that this dissonance, between stated intention and visible behavior, is one of the most common and corrosive forces inside organizations. It undermines performance, weakens commitment, and signals that the words don't mean much.

On the other hand, when leaders speak with alignment, when their framing matches what others can see and feel, trust becomes more durable. Even in systems under strain.

Interpretive leadership doesn't require a perfect message. It requires a consistent one. It requires language that can hold partial truth without collapsing under it. It asks the leader to say things like, "Here's what we're seeing today," and then show up tomorrow with a new layer, if something changes. It's not about sticking to the script. It's about staying in relationship with the moment.

That relationship matters because when people feel that the person leading them is in the work with them and not above or outside of it, they're more likely to bring their full attention. They don't waste energy guessing what's real, and they don't need to fill in gaps with assumptions. They don't feel like they're navigating alone.

That doesn't mean trust is automatic. It still takes time. It still takes repetition. It still takes care. But interpretive leadership gives people something to return to. A voice. A posture. A rhythm. Something that helps them remember what's actually unfolding, not just what they're afraid might happen.

That steadiness becomes its own kind of signal, a pattern, rather than a fixed point. Over time, people start to track it, and they notice how the leader holds the line when the situation shifts. They pay attention to how information is framed. They begin to understand the difference between a lack of answers and a lack of grounding.

That distinction matters. In moments of change, people will look for whatever seems most solid. If what they find is someone who's still paying attention and not trying to wrap things up too quickly, they will often stay close. Even if they're unsure. Even if the next step isn't clear yet. Because the presence itself becomes a form of stability.

This is what builds trust. Not certainty. Not performance. Just the quiet, repeated act of staying in it. Of noticing what's shifting. Of helping others see what's emerging. And doing it again tomorrow.

A LIFE LIVED:

Leadership and the Side Door

Years ago, when I was teaching at my first university, I started getting pulled into work that didn't fall under my job description. It wasn't dramatic. It didn't come with a title or a plan. It started with small things like serving on a committee, helping revise something that wasn't working, being asked to weigh in when something needed fresh eyes.

I didn't think much of it at the time. I just tried to stay close to the work and respond where I could. But over time, it started to shift how people saw me.

Eventually, someone said to me, "You know you're doing leadership work, right?"

I didn't know how to respond. I hadn't thought of it that way. I wasn't in a formal leadership role. I wasn't managing a team. I was teaching. I was building things. I liked being in the middle of the work, not removed from it. I didn't have a strategy for advancing. I just kept saying yes to things that felt like they needed someone to care. And I cared. That was the only real throughline.

But slowly, I started noticing how others were responding. I was being asked into conversations I hadn't been part of before. People started treating me as someone who could help make sense of what was going on. Not in a loud or directive way. More like a reference point. Someone who could say what others were sensing but hadn't yet named. And someone who wouldn't overreact when things were still unclear.

Looking back, I can see now that the leadership wasn't in solving problems. It was in staying close to what was unfolding, helping others interpret what was shifting, and not needing to rush it into form.

That's what people were responding to, even if we didn't have language for it at the time. I was creating space for something to become clearer without pretending it already was.

The trust that formed during that time didn't come from expertise. It came from presence. From being visible without trying to take over. From offering language when it helped, and being quiet when that was better.

I wasn't directing things, but I was helping others hold what was hard to see. I stayed with it long enough for the shape of the work to become clearer to me and to others.

It wasn't a promotion. It wasn't a moment. It was something that formed slowly, through consistency. Through staying close to the tension without needing to resolve it right away. Through noticing when something didn't feel right, and being willing to say that out loud, even if I didn't have a fix.

I didn't think of that as leadership at the time. I just thought I was being helpful. But now I can see that what I was doing was building a kind of shared meaning. I was offering interpretation when others felt unsure. I was helping connect the dots without claiming to see the whole picture.

I've come to believe that a lot of leadership begins that way. Not with a plan, but with attention. Not with authority, but with trust. Not with confidence, but with a willingness to be present while something takes shape.

It doesn't always look like leadership. But it holds like leadership. When the people around you feel that, they start to hold it too.

I didn't set out to lead, but in staying close to what was real, I helped others stay close too.

PUTTING IT TO WORK: THREE DIMENSIONS OF APPLICATION

Industry

In industries shaped by rapid change, leaders are often told to move quickly. To respond to market shifts. To stay ahead of competitors. But what often gets missed is the quality of attention that comes before the movement.

Leaders who make time to frame what's unfolding with presence and not with spin, create an environment where others can move with more coherence and not just faster, but better. Interpretive leadership becomes a competitive advantage because it reduces internal friction. It gives teams a shared sense of what's happening and why it matters, even before the full picture is in view. And that shared framing often holds up better than a hurried plan when the next shift comes.

Professional Career

Inside organizations, people notice who speaks with care. They notice who takes the time to name what's still in motion. Who helps others stay oriented without pretending to have it all figured out. Those are often the people others start turning to for steadiness as well as for answers.

You don't need a title to lead this way. You don't need formal authority. What you need is presence and the willingness to help others hold the shape of what's unfolding, even when it's not clear yet. Over time, those behaviors build credibility by how you move when the ground is uncertain.

Personal Life

This kind of leadership doesn't stop when the workday ends. The ability to stay in a moment that hasn't resolved itself yet and to help others name what they're experiencing without rushing them through it, is just as needed in personal relationships. With friends. With family. With people we care about who are going through change.

You don't need to fix things. You don't need to narrate someone else's story. But if you can help them stay connected to what's true, even when it's messy, slow, or painful, you're doing something that matters. You're building trust, and you're giving them space to make meaning in their own time, with someone who doesn't flinch.

5

COLLECT THE DOTS, CONNECT THE DOTS

W e usually think of leadership as having answers. Being decisive. Choosing a direction and committing to it. And that makes sense because it's often what the role seems to demand. But in practice, some of the most meaningful moments in leadership don't look like that. They show up earlier, when things are still unclear and there isn't an obvious move to make.

What ends up separating people, those who lead in a way that really matters from those who just manage the job, often has less to do with decisiveness and more to do with the way they see. It's not about predicting what's coming next. It's more about noticing what's already here. It's spotting threads that others miss and picking up on signals that don't seem to belong together yet, but might.

In most causal systems, leadership is defined by clarity, by knowing where you're headed and mapping the most efficient route to get there. But in uncertain environments, that kind of clarity often doesn't exist at the start.

"Effectual leaders" don't wait for full visibility. They move by collecting information as they go, noticing what's already present, and connecting signals others miss. This chapter explores that way of leading: one that draws strength from disciplined observation and trust in partial progress, rather than prediction.

Maybe you've heard this quote from Steve Jobs: "You can't connect the dots looking forward, you can only connect them looking backward." It gets tossed around a lot, and it can start to feel overused.

But even so, it holds something important. What he's pointing to isn't just about hindsight. It's about how meaning takes shape over time. Leadership, in a way, is less about grand gestures and more about recognizing patterns. And that only happens if you have dots to work with.

So where do those dots come from?

They come from your life. From the jobs you've held. The roles you've played. The places you've worked. The stuff that didn't go as planned. The people who taught you something, sometimes without meaning to. The frustrations you've hit up against. Maybe most of all, the things you didn't notice at first but now realize mattered.

You gather these dots as you go. Through experience. Through listening. Trying something and seeing how it feels. Getting it wrong. Paying closer attention.

Most of the time, you don't know it's a dot while it's happening. That part only clicks later. Something small like a passing comment, a tough assignment, a season of doubt: it doesn't register much at the time. But years later, it ends up shaping the way you respond. The way you lead.

That's why it's important to keep collecting. Before you can connect anything, you need enough to work with. You can't draw from an empty well. And the tricky part is, you don't get to know in advance which dots will end up mattering. So the best thing you can do is stay open. Stay curious. Pay attention, even when the moment feels ordinary.

Some people seem to know this by instinct. Entrepreneurs, especially. They build things by rearranging what's already there in ways nobody else has tried. It's not always invention. It's connection.

Think about Starbucks. Howard Schultz didn't invent coffee. He didn't invent cafés. What he did was notice how the Italian café culture made people feel. He saw the idea of a "third place" between home and work. He paid attention to consistency, to how a space could be designed to feel familiar no matter where you were. He didn't create something from scratch; what he did was gather pieces and give them a shape.

That's the kind of leadership this chapter is pointing to. Not creativity in the flashy sense. More like the quiet work of noticing and staying with what you've noticed. Leaders who do this well build a kind of inner library. A collection of things they've picked up over time. When the moment comes, especially when things feel uncertain, they have something to draw from.

When others are still looking for the right answer, they're seeing patterns take shape.

THE DISCIPLINE OF DOT COLLECTING

Most people assume that insight shows up fully formed. Great ideas arrive all at once, sparked by inspiration or genius. But in practice, insight is a *byproduct of attention*, and attention is a discipline.

Leaders who consistently generate meaningful insights, those who anticipate shifts, spot emerging needs, or reframe complexity, aren't just good at connecting ideas. They're good at collecting them. Patiently. Deliberately. And often without knowing exactly when or how those pieces will come together.

Dot collecting isn't about stockpiling knowledge or taking obsessive notes. It's about developing a habit of observation. It's about seeing beyond what's obvious and holding onto what's *curious*. It's noticing patterns in people's behavior, hearing what's not being said in a meeting, or recognizing when something doesn't quite fit, even if you can't articulate why yet.

Multi-dimensional leaders tend to notice things that others miss because they've made a habit of tuning in. They've learned to pay attention on purpose, not just when something's broken, but all the time. They're not just reacting to what's around them. They're picking up on what's under the surface. What keeps repeating. What doesn't quite line up.

They notice when a tension shows up again. Then again. Not always loudly. Sometimes it's just a recurring friction that is small but persistent. They pay attention when workarounds stop looking temporary and start becoming the way things get done. When people stop raising a concern out loud, but keep adjusting their behavior in subtle ways.

They also notice the questions that seem to hang in the air. The ones that come up, don't quite land, and quietly disappear because the room moved on. They take those moments seriously.

Informal conversations can say a lot, too. What gets shared in passing at lunch, after a meeting, in the in-between spaces often points to problems that haven't made it into a slide deck yet. These leaders listen for that. Not as gossip. Not as noise. But as a signal.

Then there are the decisions that look right on paper but feel off in practice. The ones where everything checks out, but something still doesn't sit quite right. Leaders who've developed this kind of attention don't dismiss that feeling. They sit with it. They try to understand what might be missing.

Most of all, they take note of anomalies. The exceptions. The things that don't fit. That's often where the real insight starts. Not at the center, where everything is clear and expected, but at the edges, where something different is trying to show up.

In organizational theory, these are often called *weak signals*. These are subtle, early indicators of change that are easy to overlook but often carry immense significance. Studies show that organizations able to detect and interpret weak signals are often the first to adapt or seize emerging opportunities.

But weak signals don't shout. They whisper. And only leaders who've developed the discipline of observation are prepared to hear them.

Dot collecting also requires a degree of humility. It means acknowledging that we don't always know what matters in the moment. Not every meeting or interaction will reveal its value right away. But by staying alert and by observing without judgment, we start to see threads we wouldn't have noticed otherwise.

This kind of attention also lays the groundwork for *pattern recognition*, a skill strongly associated with expert leadership and strategic decision-making. Research into high-level executive behavior shows that experienced leaders often make complex decisions not by running through exhaustive analysis, but by recognizing familiar structures in unfamiliar situations. What looks like intuition is actually accumulated exposure. It's pattern memory.

The more diverse the exposure is, the more valuable the dots become. Studies in adaptive leadership and cross-sector learning show that exposure diversity, working across different functions, industries, or disciplines, increases the likelihood of breakthrough thinking. Each new perspective adds a layer to your mental archive, giving you more to draw from when insight is needed most.

Over time, this kind of disciplined attention creates its own momentum. We begin to build a personal archive of ideas, tensions, and patterns, some active, some dormant, that we can draw from when the moment is right.

Dot collecting is not an act of passivity. It's an act of leadership. It's preparation.

It's what makes insight possible when others are still searching for inspiration.

HOW LEADERS COLLECT AND CONNECT THE DOTS

COLLECTING THE DOTS

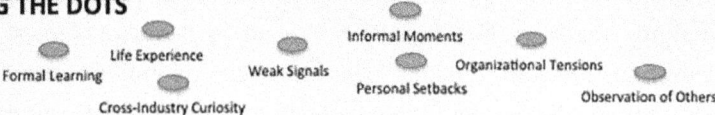

Informal Moments

Life Experience

Formal Learning　　　Weak Signals　　Organizational Tensions

Personal Setbacks

Cross-Industry Curiosity　　　　　　　Observation of Others

Framing | Pattern Recognition | Pause for Meaning

CONNECTING THE DOTS

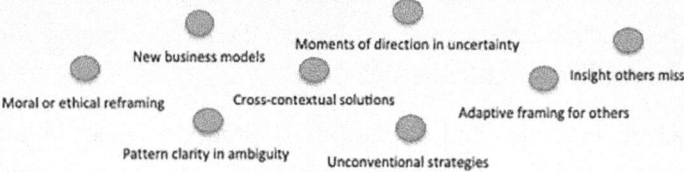

Moments of direction in uncertainty

New business models

Insight others miss

Moral or ethical reframing　　Cross-contextual solutions

Adaptive framing for others

Pattern clarity in ambiguity　　Unconventional strategies

Figure 5: This visual shows how leaders gather raw inputs over time and then transform them into insight through framing, pattern recognition, and reflection. Insight isn't found—it's formed.

FROM EXPOSURE TO INSIGHT:
TURNING EXPERIENCE INTO MEANINGFUL ACTION

Leadership insight doesn't arrive fully formed—it's built. This diagram traces the hidden process many leaders move through without realizing it: collecting dots from everyday experience, then connecting those dots through pattern recognition and reflection.

The upper half of the visual represents the exposure phase; those moments that don't always feel significant at the time. Life experience, weak signals, organizational tension, and personal setbacks accumulate quietly, often unnoticed. They become the raw material for future insight.

The lower half captures the transition to meaning. Insight emerges not from more data, but from pausing to frame what those experiences might mean. This is where leaders begin to connect the dots—seeing new strategies, finding clarity in ambiguity, or offering adaptive framing to others.

This process is not linear. It requires time, humility, and often distance. But for leaders who learn to pause and reflect, the result is a kind of insight that others often miss.

REFLECTION PROMPT

Think of a time when a past experience, something that didn't seem important at the time, suddenly helped you see a current situation more clearly.

- What "dot" were you finally connecting?

- What helped the connection emerge?

- How might you make more space in your life to notice and name the dots as they appear?

THE SKILL OF CONNECTION

Collecting dots creates potential. Connecting them creates value.

But connection isn't just a creative act. It's a skill. A kind of discipline. One that's shaped by practice, timing, and a certain comfort with uncertainty. And sometimes, a willingness to speak up before everything is fully clear.

This is where many leaders get stuck. They collect the dots. They sense that something is forming. That there's meaning there. But they hesitate. They wait for more data. They wait for someone else to validate the insight because they don't trust what they see.

That hesitation is understandable. Most of us have been taught to hold off until something feels complete. Until we can prove it. We're used to showing up with answers, not with emerging patterns.

But connection often happens before confirmation. It asks you to step forward with something that might still be incomplete. It asks you to draw a line, even when the surety isn't there, because you're starting to see something. And even that small move, saying, "I think there might be something here," can change the conversation.

Psychologists talk about the "eureka gap," the lag between when insight shows up in the brain and when we're able to put it into words. During that gap, a lot can get lost. Leaders might sense something important, but without the language to explain it, they hold back. They move on. And the moment passes.

That's called pattern suppression. It happens quietly. Often, it comes from fear of being early or being dismissed before the thought has a chance to land.

Still, this is what effective leadership often requires. Being willing to voice something before it's fully formed to surface a possibility and to say, "This isn't polished yet, but it feels like it matters."

That kind of move is rooted in perspective-taking. The ability to shift the frame. To look at something familiar from a new angle. It's not about having a better answer. It's about holding the question differently. Leaders who connect dots well tend to do this. They ask, "What if this isn't about efficiency at all?" or "Could this issue be a signal from somewhere else in the system?"

Sometimes, all it takes is that shift, a reframing of the conversation that makes something click simply because someone saw the facts differently.

This isn't just about ideas. Connecting dots often means connecting people. Someone in marketing hears a complaint that someone in operations has already solved. Someone in finance is asking a question that customers have been answering for months. These dots live in different parts of the system. The leader who can see the connection and name it often moves the organization forward without needing authority to do it.

Dot connecting isn't about being brilliant. It's about being present. It's about seeing what's already there and giving it shape in a way others can act on.

It's how observation becomes insight.

And how insight becomes motion.

BARRIERS TO CONNECTING

If connecting the dots is such a powerful leadership skill, why don't more people do it? Why do so many good ideas stay buried, and why are some of the most insightful perspectives never voiced?

The answer isn't a lack of intelligence or effort. It's friction, structural, psychological, and cultural. More often than not, the greatest friction comes not from real constraints, but **imagined ones**, the internal narratives we absorb over time that quietly narrow our field of vision.

1. Cognitive Barriers

If connecting the dots is such a powerful skill and one that can lead to insight, alignment, and even real change, then it's fair to ask why it doesn't happen more often. Why some ideas stay buried. Why a pattern someone notices never makes it into the room. Why a good instinct doesn't become action.

The answer usually isn't effort. It's not intelligence either. Most people are paying attention in their own way. The challenge is that there's friction. Some of it's structural. Some of it's internal. A lot of it lives in the culture.

The friction sometimes doesn't come from real constraints. It comes from imagined ones, quiet stories we absorb over time that shape what we think we're allowed to say, notice, or share.

Many of these hesitations are symptoms of overly causal environments where the expectation is to show up with answers, not questions. But in uncertain systems, those instincts often suppress the very insights that are most needed.

Environments that overvalue planning and proof can end up undervaluing perception and pattern recognition, which are critical in fast-changing systems.

We want things to make sense. It's natural. The brain is wired to find order, to resolve ambiguity. When we come across something that doesn't fit, the instinct is often to explain it away. To smooth it over. This is what psychologists call "confirmation bias": we look for what supports what we already believe and filter out what doesn't.

Sometimes we stop looking too soon. Once we find an answer that seems good enough, we settle. That's called "premature cognitive closure." It means we miss what might still be unfolding. We miss the connections that live between ideas that are not fully resolved, but are worth sitting with.

Even when we do spot a pattern, we might not trust ourselves. We've been trained to value certainty, so anything partial feels risky. If something doesn't come with proof, we keep it to ourselves. Over time, those hesitations become habits. *I probably don't have enough to go on. Someone else must have already thought of it. It's not my place to bring it up.*

Those aren't rules. But they feel like rules. And they're strong enough to stop something important from taking shape.

2. Social Risk

In a lot of environments, especially high-performing ones, the cost of being wrong can feel bigger than the value of being early. Suggesting a connection that isn't obvious might make you sound off-base or disruptive. Even if the idea is useful, the timing might feel off. So people hold back.

They learn to wait until things are more polished. More proven. But by then, the window to act might be gone, and the people who had something to say don't feel quite as safe saying it the next time.

This kind of hesitancy adds up. Over time, it starts to erode trust. Not the obvious kind, the deeper kind. People stop testing ideas out loud. They stop thinking together. Eventually, they stop looking for patterns at all.

The research backs this up. Psychological safety, the sense that you can share an idea without being dismissed or judged, is one of the strongest predictors of whether teams surface insight. If people feel like early thoughts will be punished, they stop sharing early thoughts. It's not just about what's said. It's about what never gets said.

That tone is set by leaders. If you want people to make connections, they have to know it's okay to show up with something half-formed. They have to hear others say, "I'm not sure yet, but this feels important," and watch that be treated as valuable. You don't create safety by encouraging risk. You create it by making room for uncertainty.

3. Siloed Contexts

Sometimes the dots don't get connected because they live in different places, and the people holding them don't talk to each other. Marketing doesn't know what customer service is hearing. Product isn't in the room for financial planning. Senior leaders might never see the raw feedback from the frontline.

It's not that the connections aren't there because they are. It's that no one's in position to notice them. Or the system doesn't make it easy to share them.

Even here, imagined constraints play a role. That's not my team. I don't want to step on toes. We've always done it this way. No one says those things directly. But they shape how people move, and what they believe they're allowed to name.

Multi-dimensional leaders work across those lines by translating across them. They listen for what one group sees that another might be missing. They help make sense of it in a shared language. That's often what unlocks something. Not expertise. Just proximity to the pattern.

4. The Myth of the Big Idea

Then there's the myth that leadership means showing up with something brilliant. That a real contribution has to be bold and finished and undeniable.

But most meaningful insights start small. They begin with noticing. Following a thread. Offering a thought that isn't quite there yet.

If people think they need a big idea to speak up, they'll wait. They'll try to make it perfect before they share it. In doing that, they often miss the moment.

This is where another kind of pressure shows up, what researchers call evaluative pressure. The feeling that whatever you say has to be right the first time. If that's the expectation, people get quieter. Not just out loud. In their thinking.

But big ideas don't usually come fully formed. They emerge slowly. Dot by dot. And they only take shape if there's space to work them out in real time.

So, if connecting is part of leadership, then clearing the way for others to connect is part of it too. That means noticing where the friction is and doing the work to lower it. It means creating conditions where people don't need certainty to contribute, and early insight is seen as valuable. Where making sense of something together is part of the job, not something extra.

Because the more people feel free to notice, the more a team can see.

And the more they see, the more they can shape.

CREATING THE CONDITIONS

The ability to connect dots isn't just a personal skill. It's something broader than that. It becomes part of the culture. Like most cultural capacities, it doesn't just happen. It has to be made possible.

Multi-dimensional leaders don't just connect the dots themselves. They create the conditions for others to do it too. They understand that pattern recognition doesn't come from pressure. It comes from permission. And the kind of permission that matters here isn't formal, it's usually unspoken. It's in how space is held. How questions are asked. How unfinished thoughts are received.

In high-performing environments, especially where everything runs tight, attention tends to get funneled toward what's measurable. Metrics, timelines, deliverable, and the focus narrows.

When that happens, the space for observation, a real observation, starts to shrink. People stop noticing. Not because they don't care, but because there's no oxygen left for it.

Good leaders reverse that. They don't just say "Pay attention." They show what it looks like. They ask different kinds of questions. They slow down enough to notice things out loud. They make it normal to speak up even when the insight isn't polished yet. Especially then.

They reward early noticing. They treat questions as valuable even if there's no clear next step. They give weight to a quiet observation, even if it doesn't tie back to a KPI. They know that insight usually arrives in pieces, and if you wait for the whole thing to appear, you've already missed it.

There's research behind this. Studies on organizational learning show that the strongest predictor of whether insight and innovation take root is psychological safety. That means: can people speak up without fear? Can they share something they're wondering about, even if it's not fully thought through? Can they ask questions that might not have answers yet?

In teams where the answer is yes, more dots get collected, more connections get made, and more possibilities start to open up.

This is especially true in complex systems and environments where no one person holds all the information and where the work crosses functions, roles, and levels.

In places like that, the leaders who make the most progress aren't the ones with the strongest opinions. They're the ones who create visibility. They're the ones who ask what people are noticing as opposed to what they are doing. What's not sitting right. What seems to be changing.

They also build simple ways to make connection easier. These don't need to be big shifts. They just need to be deliberate.

They might:

- Create opportunities for teams that don't usually interact to talk to each other
- Include frontline voices in strategic conversations
- Invite people to share early-stage thinking, not just finished plans
- Ask what feels off, not just what's on track
- Frame anomalies as something to explore, not something to fix

These small moves matter. Research on how groups think and learn shows that the shape of a conversation and its openness, as well as how it invites participation, can matter more than the content itself. When boundaries are porous and the cost of early contribution is low, the group becomes more adaptive. People see more, and they say more.

That kind of culture makes insight more likely. But more than that, it builds something deeper, a shared sense that learning is valid. That insight doesn't have to be predictive. It can be built in motion. It can emerge in real time.

Leaders who understand this take responsibility for modeling it. They don't just celebrate ideas. They show how ideas come together. They share the dots they're connecting. They think out loud. They reflect in the open so that others see how clarity is made.

Connecting dots isn't just something you do. It's something people see you do.

And once they see it, they can start doing it too.

A LIFE LIVED:

Connecting the Dots on Purpose

When I look back at my path from standing behind the counter at my parents' camera shop at eight years old to teaching in an Ivy League institution, it's not a straight line. Honestly, it barely looks like a line at all. If you only saw the endpoints, it might seem like a leap. I get why people who've known me for a long time still ask how it all fits together.

But from where I sit, it doesn't feel disconnected.

To me, it looks more like a series of dots. Each one real. Each one meaningful. I didn't know how they'd link up at the time. There was no plan. No long arc. It was more like hopping rocks in a stream. You don't always know where the next one is until you need it. You land where you can, you steady yourself, and then you look for the next.

A colleague once said it reminded him of rock climbing in that you can only ever see a few holds ahead, and then you have to trust your way up. That felt right. I've thought about that a lot.

For a while, that was my story. The dots connected after the fact. The meaning came later.

But at some point, something shifted. I don't know exactly when, but I remember the moment that sparked it. It was that quote from Steve Jobs, the one about how you can only connect the dots looking backward. I'd heard it before. A lot of people have. But this time it landed differently. It made me pause.

What it helped me realize was that the dots themselves weren't random. They were experiences. Once I saw them that way, something opened up.

I started collecting dots on purpose.

I began looking for experiences that might expand my lens. I followed threads even when I didn't know where they were going. I started paying closer attention to the patterns I kept encountering. Some of it was deliberate. Some of it just unfolded. But I was more aware of what I was noticing and why it might matter later.

It happened in my business life, too. I bought my parents' photography retail store because it felt like the right next step and not part of some grand plan. I'd grown up in that space. I knew the rhythms of it. I understood what it meant to work the counter, troubleshoot equipment, and talk to customers about what they were trying to capture.

But taking over the business didn't just teach me how to run a store. It taught me how to read a system. Where the bottlenecks were. What the margins looked like. How decisions, big and small, ripple through teams, vendors, and customers. It taught me how to lead in the context of constraints.

That one move became the beginning of something much larger. From that foundation, I stepped into commercial real estate, then into digital printing. Eventually into venture capital. Then hospitality.

In each shift, it wasn't about starting over, it was about building forward. I wasn't changing direction as much as I was adding dimension. Every new space gave me more dots to carry. More systems to notice. More people to learn from.

Leading in those environments felt different than teaching or writing, but it came from the same place. Paying attention. Being willing to act before everything was clear. Knowing that a decision, even when it's uncertain, can still be grounded if it's connected to something true. I made mistakes. I learned by doing. I followed hunches. And over time, I got better at seeing which dots to trust.

A good example is this book. The parts that draw on psychology, cognition, and uncertainty aren't just references. They're dots I went looking for. I didn't have formal training in those areas, but I sensed that something important lived there. So I followed that. I read deeply in academic journals. I talked to people in other fields. I sat with ideas I didn't fully understand yet. It changed how I think about leadership, especially in uncertain conditions.

Culture was another one. I've taught in twenty-two countries across five continents, and it isn't because I was chasing travel, it was because I noticed a gap. A lot of conversations around innovation and leadership were missing the role of culture and how it shapes what we notice, what we act on, and what we even consider possible.

I didn't want to just study that. I wanted to feel it. I wanted to live in systems that worked differently from the ones I knew. And doing that has changed the way I teach. The way I listen. The way I see the world.

The dots are everywhere. Some show up when you're not looking for them. Others, you have to go out and find. But in either case, the work is the same. You notice. You stay with it. You learn to trust what you're carrying, even if it hasn't taken shape yet.

That's what leadership often looks like. Not drawing the whole map up front, but learning to read the terrain as you go.

PUTTING IT TO WORK: THREE DIMENSIONS OF APPLICATION

Some of this may already sound familiar because you've lived it in some form. Most people have. That's the point. This way of seeing, collecting, connecting, and making meaning is already part of how we move through the world. Leadership just asks us to do it more deliberately and to make space for others to do it too.

There's no formula here. But if you're trying to apply these ideas, it can help to look through a few different lenses. Not as steps. Just as places to start noticing.

Industry

In fast-changing industries or any environment with complexity, insight often comes less from analysis and more from connection. Noticing what's already there. Reframing what's already known. When things are moving quickly, the differentiator usually isn't who has the best data. It's who sees the pattern first.

If your organization is navigating change, the people who can spot weak signals and draw from different parts of the system will be the ones who create opportunity. They won't always be the loudest or the most senior. But they'll be the ones who've been paying attention.

You don't have to invent something new. Often, the right move is already in the system but not seen that way yet. So instead of asking, "What's the strategy?" it might be more useful to ask, "What don't we realize we know yet?"

Professional Career

Careers are often shaped to look linear. Certain roles, certain credentials, certain steps that signal progress. But some of the strongest paths are more layered than that. What sets people apart usually isn't just what they've done, it's what they've carried with them. What they've noticed. What they've combined.

If you look back on your work, ask: *What dots have I already collected? What keeps showing up in different contexts? What have I lived through that might hold more meaning than I realized at the time?*

You might not see a full picture. That's okay. You don't have to. Often, it's better not to. What matters is continuing to collect. Continuing to trust that the next dot will make the others make more sense. You don't need certainty. You just need motion.

Personal Life

Your life holds its own archive. Relationships. Setbacks. Repeated themes. Moments that felt small but show up now in the way you make decisions or respond to others.

If you pay attention to what lingers and what energizes you, what drains you, what you keep circling back to, those patterns can shift how you understand yourself. Sometimes, that's enough to shift everything else.

Not every step needs to be strategic. Some of the best decisions you'll make in your life won't come from a plan. They'll come from reaching for something before you know exactly where it leads, trusting that if you keep showing up with your eyes open, the next rock will be there when you need it.

Note: *In all three dimensions (industry, career, and personal life), the capacity to collect and connect dots is a deeply effectual behavior. It's how leaders build direction from ambiguity and shape forward progress without waiting for the whole path to appear.*

Instead of asking, "What's the best path to get there?" they start with, "What do I already have to work with, and what can I try now?" That orientation, especially in leadership, makes all the difference when clarity is in short supply.

6

THE LOYAL REBEL

L eadership is often described in terms of vision. The ability to see ahead. To chart a path. But the harder part, the one that doesn't get talked about as much, is the part that comes after that. Acting on the vision, especially when the system isn't quite ready for it. That's where it usually gets harder. That's also where it starts to matter more.

Some of the most effective leaders I've seen aren't the ones with the clearest authority. They're not the ones making declarations at the top or the ones trying to tear everything down from the outside. They're the ones in between. People who know the system from the inside and feel the pressure to keep things going, while also sensing what needs to change.

These are the "Loyal Rebels."

Loyal Rebels don't challenge for the sake of it. They stay connected to the mission, even as they push against how it's being carried out. They care about the work and the people doing it. They believe the system can be better.

That belief doesn't make the work easier. It makes it harder. They're not standing apart from the organization, they're standing inside it, holding up a mirror.

It's a strange place to lead from. You're trying to help something grow while it's still deciding whether it wants to change. You're loyal, but you don't agree with everything. You see what could be better, but you also see why it hasn't changed yet. When you speak up, it's not to criticize from a distance, it's to stay in the tension long enough to make something shift.

This kind of leadership doesn't usually get recognized. It's not dramatic. It's not loud. Sometimes it's invisible. Sometimes it's punished. But it's needed. Especially in places where things aren't black and white. Where authority is spread out. Where uncertainty is high. Where the usual playbook stops working.

Loyal Rebels don't stand out because they have bold ideas. They stand out because they act on those ideas. Carefully. Relationally. Sometimes quietly. They connect things others haven't connected yet. They ask the harder questions. They take the risk of being early, or misunderstood, or alone.

Even when it's slow.

Even when it's not safe.

Even when it comes at a cost.

This chapter is about that kind of leadership.

The kind that stays.

The kind that challenges without leaving.

The kind that leads from the middle and keeps hold of itself in the process.

THE ANATOMY OF A LOYAL REBEL

Being a Loyal Rebel isn't about having a contrarian streak. It's about holding two truths in tension: commitment to the organization and commitment to change. Most people choose one or the other. Loyal Rebels choose both.

That duality is what gives them power and makes their position difficult to hold. They are constantly walking a leadership tightrope:

- They're insiders, but they often think like outsiders.
- They support the mission, but question the method.
- They respect authority, but don't defer to it blindly.
- They understand the rules, but are willing to challenge them when they no longer serve.

This balancing act isn't a weakness. It's a skill. Many organizations quietly depend on it, even if they rarely acknowledge it.

Research in organizational behavior confirms what many Loyal Rebels experience. Meaningful change is most often driven by people embedded within the system who act on what they see. It is a misnomer to think it is driven by top-down mandates or outside disruption.

These leaders operate in what some researchers describe as "boundary-spanning roles." That is, they move across silos, interpret strategy, and bring together perspectives that usually stay separate. They don't push for revolution; they work toward slow evolution.

That kind of leadership matters most in systems built for stability. Most organizations are designed to manage risk, protect efficiency, and keep things moving. That usually means reinforcing the status quo. Over time, those systems can get very good at repeating what works and less able to notice when what works has stopped being relevant.

That's where Loyal Rebels come in.

They tend to be early recognizers. They sense misalignments, emerging shifts, and slow drift before the rest of the system catches up. They see the signal in the noise. And because they've earned credibility inside the system, they're able to raise concerns, shift conversations, or take action, sometimes before the formal strategy does.

But insight isn't enough. What this role really requires is emotional stamina and political fluency. Change involves people, and people bring their own history, fears, pressures, and beliefs to the table. Loyal Rebels don't push through that. They work with it. They move through relation-ships, not around them.

That's what makes them valuable. It's also what makes them vulnerable.

They understand what it costs to be early. They know what happens when you challenge too soon or in the wrong way. They know that credibility is what makes dissent possible. They know how quickly trust can be lost if the challenge doesn't land.

Timing matters. So does tone. So does knowing the room.

This chapter explores how Loyal Rebels manage that. How they hold their stance. How they navigate the tension of pushing forward while staying inside. How they build trust, protect relationships, and stay grounded in values they're not willing to give up.

Because the goal isn't disruption for its own sake.

The goal is to help the system see itself clearly enough to change.

CREDIBILITY BEFORE CHALLENGE

In most organizations, challenge without credibility is easy to ignore. But credibility without challenge can turn into quiet compliance.

Loyal Rebels understand this. They know that if their insights are going to matter, if their dissent is going to carry weight, it has to come from a place of earned trust. Trust doesn't come from having a title. It comes from how people experience you over time.

Credibility isn't about being liked. It's about being trusted for your intent and respected for your judgment. People don't have to agree with you. But if they believe you're acting in good faith on behalf of something larger than yourself, they're more likely to listen.

Influence doesn't get handed to you. You build it. Through how you show up, what you contribute, and the patterns you create. Over time, those patterns start to matter more than your position.

Loyal Rebels tend to earn that influence in a few quiet, consistent ways.

They deliver.

Before they challenge anything, they establish reliability. They follow through. They meet expectations. They become known for competence. This builds the foundation that makes their insights easier to hear.

They listen before they lead.

They take time to understand the system as it is. They try to understand why decisions have been made, what assumptions are at play, and what language the organization uses to make sense of itself. They learn the rules before they question them.

They link their ideas to shared goals.

They frame their observations around what the organization already says it values, like customer experience, operational quality, team well-being, and ethics. When a challenge is anchored in the mission, it's easier to receive. It feels like part of the work, not a threat to it.

This is how credibility becomes influence. Slowly. Through relationship, through repetition, through alignment.

Once that foundation is in place, Loyal Rebels gain something essential; the ability to speak truth without being immediately seen as opposition.

That's when challenge starts to move.

THE PRACTICE OF STRATEGIC DISSENT

Strategic dissent isn't about being right. It's about being effective.

There's a difference. You can have a valid point, but if the way you express it shuts people down, the insight won't land. Loyal Rebels learn that early. They figure out how to speak up in ways that protect both the relationship and the truth by learning how and when to bring it forward.

Research backs this up. People tend to be more open to challenge when it's offered through care, not critique. It doesn't mean you avoid hard truths. It means you take care in how you surface them. You stay mindful of what the relationship can hold.

That care shows up in small choices:

They choose the right moment: even a well-formed idea will fall flat if the timing is wrong. Strategic dissent is about more than content, it's about emotional and political awareness. Not everything needs to be said right away.

They lead with curiosity: questions create more space than statements. Certainty tends to shut doors. A better question often does more than a strong opinion.

They name the tension, not the person: feedback that focuses on patterns or gaps invites participation, while feedback that centers on individuals often leads to defensiveness.

They offer a path forward: even if it's not complete. Even if it's just a possibility. The gesture matters. Offering a way forward helps others stay open.

They model the tone: Loyal Rebels pay attention to their posture. They show it's possible to dissent without disrespect. Calm can still carry conviction. Disagreement doesn't have to escalate.

When this is done well, dissent doesn't feel like conflict. It feels like stewardship. A way of taking care. A way of holding the system accountable to what it says it wants to be.

RECOGNIZING LOYAL REBELS IN THE SYSTEM

Loyal Rebels don't always announce themselves. You won't always find them at the front of the room. Some of the most valuable ones move quietly, testing ideas, building trust, and shaping the system from within.

They often don't carry formal power. They rarely ask for recognition. But their impact adds up over time, and part of the work of leadership is learning to notice that.

It's also learning to tell the difference.

Not all dissent looks the same. Some challenge because they care. Others challenge because they're frustrated, or misaligned, or trying to meet a different need. That distinction matters. Not because one is always right and the other is always wrong but because they create very different ripple effects.

Organizational research has drawn this line for years. It distinguishes between two kinds of voice: "prohibitive" and "promotive."

Prohibitive voice is when someone speaks up to stop something. It usually comes from a place of concern or caution, calling out a risk, an inefficiency, or a breakdown. It's protective, and sometimes it's necessary. Prohibitive voice can keep teams from heading in the wrong direction. But on its own, it doesn't usually move things forward.

Promotive voice, on the other hand, is about building. It's when people speak up to improve how things work to suggest a better approach, name a missed opportunity, or reframe a challenge. It's not just about what's wrong. It's about what's possible. It tends to be the kind of voice most closely linked to innovation, learning, and long-term trust.

In practical terms, that means leaders need a way to recognize the intent behind the dissent and to support it when it's coming from a place of grounded contribution. One helpful tool for this is what we call the "Credibility Compass." Not a formula. Not a label. Just a set of patterns to watch for. A way to stay attentive to whether someone's voice is building toward something or just pushing against it.

But recognition is only the first step.

Loyal Rebels are most effective when leaders do more than tolerate them, and they find ways to bring them closer to the work of shaping change. Studies on "disciplined employees," those who demonstrate both loyalty to the system and a strong sense of personal accountability, suggest that organizations perform better when they give these individuals room to act. Not unbounded freedom but clear boundaries and real influence.

THE CREDIBILITY COMPASS		
Dimension	Loyal Rebel	Disruptive Dissenter
Intention	Aims to improve outcomes for the team or mission	Aims for control, recognition, or emotional release
Track Record	Known for follow-through and adding value	Known for friction, blame, or unresolved conflict
Timing	Raises issues when they're likely to be heard	Speaks up regardless of readiness or capacity
Alternatives	Offers options or reframes the problem	Fixates on flaws without offering a way forward
Relational Posture	Challenges ideas while protecting relationships	Makes it personal or adversarial
Engagement	Stays involved, even when disagreed with	Disengages or withdraws if not validated

Disciplined contributors often thrive when they're trusted with hard problems. When they're brought into early conversations. When they're asked not just to execute, but to help reframe.

These aren't people who need constant oversight. They need clarity about where they can lead, and permission to do it in ways that might feel unconventional.

This doesn't require a formal program. It requires attention. Leaders can start by:

- Noticing where friction is coming from and whether it's attached to care
- Creating spaces where it's safe to raise tensions before they harden into conflict
- Inviting Loyal Rebels into decision-making earlier, especially when stakes are high
- Assigning them to boundary roles, where cross-functional insight is essential
- Giving them sponsors or allies inside the system who can amplify their contributions

Perhaps most importantly, by naming their value. Out loud. In rooms where others can hear it.

You don't need a diagnostic tool to find a Loyal Rebel. But you do need to pay attention to the long arc of someone's impact. Look for contribution that holds, even in discomfort. Look for someone who keeps showing up when it would be easier not to.

Ask yourself: *Does this person make the system better, even when it's inconvenient?*

If the answer is yes, they're someone worth protecting. Someone worth inviting in more deeply before the system really needs them.

You could also think of Loyal Rebels as a lived expression of multi-dimensional leadership. They carry more than one lens at a time. They move between roles, priorities, and ways of thinking without needing to collapse into one position. That's part of what gives them their strength and also what makes the work exhausting.

Multi-dimensional leaders don't just span departments. They span values. They span timelines. They hold both what is and what could be. Loyal Rebels do that almost every day. They hold their care for the system and their discomfort with it. They stay loyal without going quiet. They stay critical without pulling away. They're translating across those layers constantly because they feel responsible to and not because someone told them to.

So if you're looking for multi-dimensional leadership in your organization, start by looking for the Loyal Rebels.

When you find them, don't just listen to what they're saying. Pay attention to what they're holding.

Ask yourself:

- *Who are the Loyal Rebels in your world?*
- *Whose voice has been steady, even when it was inconvenient?*
- *Who has been holding tension and not just pointing it out?*
- *Have you created enough space for them to stay in the work, or have they had to carry it alone?*

If you're trying to grow multi-dimensional leadership, start with the ones already doing it.

THE EMOTIONAL COST OF LEADING FROM THE MIDDLE

Loyal Rebels tend to carry more than one role at once. They hold tension between competing demands, loyalty to the system and challenge to its current state, care for people and pressure to deliver, and visibility without full authority. Over time, that tension creates a specific kind of strain.

This is the emotional cost of leading from the middle.

Recent research from Harvard Business School and the Center for Creative Leadership suggests that mid-level leaders experience some of the highest levels of emotional labor in the organizational hierarchy. They're expected to interpret strategy from the top, translate it into action on the ground, and navigate upward and downward influence, often in the same conversation.

What makes this hard isn't just the complexity. It's the emotional residue they carry from both directions. They're absorbing pressure from above and below, and are still expected to stay steady.

A 2020 study published in the *Academy of Management Journal* found that people in "in-between" roles, those without formal power but with high levels of accountability, report more role conflict, more identity strain, and more chronic ambiguity than either senior executives or frontline staff.

This isn't just about workload. It's something deeper. A kind of emotional whiplash: being seen as both insider and outsider, advocate and enforcer, change-maker and stabilizer. Often all at once.

Organizational theory has long recognized these roles as boundary-spanning: positions that sit between groups, functions, or power centers. While these roles are essential to adaptability, they come with a quiet cost.

People in these roles are constantly translating. Constantly filtering. Constantly adjusting how they show up based on the room they're in. Over time, that creates strain. Not always visible but cumulative.

Studies in emotional labor have shown that when people are asked to regulate their expression in high-pressure environments, especially without structural support, it leads to burnout in less visible ways.

Not the kind that results in someone walking out. The kind where someone stays but slowly withdraws. They stay in the job, but stop offering the insight that used to set them apart. They stop asking the harder questions. Not because they've stopped caring, but because they've stopped believing it will change anything.

This is one of the real risks of leading from the middle. I don't mean burnout, I mean *futility*. That slow drift from engaged participation to quiet disengagement. It can happen even to the most committed, most capable leaders. Especially when they've carried complexity alone for too long.

The most effective leaders I've worked with are the ones who know how to see this. They don't just ask how someone is performing. They listen for what it's costing them. They notice when someone's contribution is still strong, but their presence has shifted. They understand that people who lead from the middle are often absorbing the system's contradictions, and that kind of work doesn't just need strategy. It needs care.

Not protection.

Not rescue.

Just the awareness that staying in complexity is harder than it looks.

STAYING GROUNDED: IDENTITY AND ENERGY IN THE MIDDLE

The work of a Loyal Rebel is rarely fast. It's not loud. It's not linear. Most of the time, it's repetitive. Quiet. Sometimes invisible.

If that work isn't protected, if it isn't supported by something deeper, it starts to wear people down. Even the most committed leaders can lose their footing without practices that help them return to center. Without that, it's easy to slip from resilience into erosion.

That's why staying grounded isn't just personal, it's strategic. It's part of what makes long-term leadership possible.

Researchers at the University of Pennsylvania's Positive Psychology Center describe resilience as the capacity to recover well. To reframe what's hard. To stay rooted in your values even when the pressure keeps coming. It has little to do with pushing through stress.

That framing matters because for Loyal Rebels, the pressure doesn't go away. The ambiguity doesn't resolve. The strain doesn't wait until you're ready. So, staying grounded can't be something you do when things settle. It has to be part of how you lead.

A multi-year study by McKinsey & Company found that leaders who sustain resilience over time tend to lean on three things: clarity of purpose, emotional regulation, and strong relational networks. Not as add-ons. As essentials. Especially for people who are trying to lead without the protection of formal authority.

In practice, that looks like a few things. Not dramatic. But consistent.

- **Anchoring in purpose.** Not role. Not status. Not approval. Just the deeper *why* behind why you're in the work. When feedback is inconsistent or absent, purpose becomes the thing that steadies you. Research on psychological resilience shows that people who can name their core motivations are more likely to keep going, even when the path is uncertain. Especially when they're standing alone.

- **Pacing intensity.** Pressure doesn't always come in waves. Sometimes it's constant. If you're always running at full tilt, burnout doesn't feel like collapse; it feels like numbness. Loyal Rebels who last learn how to shift gears. They know when to lean in and when to step back. When to speak, and when to listen. They don't treat rest like a reward. They treat it like part of the work.

- **Holding a broader sense of self.** They stay connected to who they are outside the system through relationships, creative work, physical practices, anything that reminds them they're more than the role they're playing. Behavioral research calls this a "multi-self" identity. It's associated with better well-being, more adaptability, and less vulnerability to role-based stress. You can give yourself fully to the work without letting it consume your sense of who you are.

- **Finding someone else who understands.** Not a crowd. Not a coach. Just someone who gets it. Who knows what it feels like to hold complexity and not give up. Studies on workplace belonging show that even one trusted relationship can significantly increase resilience, especially in ambiguous or high-stakes environments. Loyal Rebels don't need constant affirmation, but they do need not to feel alone.

- **Treating sustainability as part of the mission.** They don't frame recovery as self-care. They frame it as staying able to lead because the goal isn't to be the one who burns the brightest. The goal is to still be in the work when the system is finally ready to change. Most transformation doesn't happen in a moment. It happens through many small acts, held over time, by people who chose not to give up too soon.

LEADING WITH ONE FOOT IN

Loyal Rebels rarely get a clear invitation. They don't usually get formal authority. Most of the time, they don't get full alignment either. They lead anyway.

But the way they lead is different. It's not all-in in the usual sense. It's not checked out either. It's something in between.

They lead with one foot in.

One foot in the system. One foot in what's possible. One foot in what is. One foot in what could be.

This doesn't mean they're undecided. It means they're holding both. They care about where the system is trying to go, and they care about how it's working now. They don't reject the present, and they don't overreach into the future. They stay connected to both, which is part of what gives their leadership its depth and its difficulty.

You won't always recognize it as leadership. It doesn't come with a title or a platform. It comes in quieter ways, through the questions they ask, the tensions they name, the way they stay when it would be easier to leave.

They don't lead through force. They lead through presence. Through relationship. Through timing.

They don't push trust. They build it. Slowly. Enough that, when they finally speak into something, people listen differently.

They don't try to control change. They try to make it possible.

They don't wait for full permission to act. They look for small openings and use them. They work from the middle because it's where both the problem and the potential tend to live.

Loyal Rebels lead with one foot in, and one foot forward.

It's not the easiest place to stand. But it's often where real change begins.

Not from the outside.

Not from the top.

From the people willing to stay in the complexity and still move.

A LIFE LIVED:

Earning My Way In - One Conversation At A Time

At the time I'm writing this, I'm involved in six different organizations. Two that I operate on my own. One I co-own with my wife. And three that live inside higher education: two universities, and a smaller unit nested inside one of them.

It's not a plan I designed. It's just what has taken shape over time. What it's given me is an ongoing, real-time look at how leadership and culture actually work across systems. Not in theory, but in the texture of meetings and decisions and relationships. Without setting out to, I've found myself living out the Loyal Rebel dynamic in ways that are both energizing and, if I'm honest, exhausting.

It's different in the spaces I've built myself. In the companies I run, there's nothing to rebel against when you're the one who shaped the system.

In the business I share with my wife, while we bring different perspectives, we've had years to figure out how we work. We know each other's rhythms. We trust each other's roles. Disagreement still happens, but it's low-stakes. It stays constructive.

But institutions are different, especially academic ones.

I've spent decades working inside higher education. Teaching. Advising. Building programs. But I've never pursued tenure. That was a choice I made years ago, when I left my PhD program to build businesses instead.

I don't carry any resentment about that decision. I respect the colleagues who've followed that path, and I understand what the structure is meant to protect. But the reality is: I'll never hold the institutional power that comes with that title. I won't be the person with the final word. And I'm okay with that.

What I've come to learn is that influence often travels further than authority if it's earned. I've also learned that influence always starts with credibility.

The two universities I'm involved with offer an interesting contrast. Both serve similar missions. But the way they think about influence, the way they make space for voices, is different.

At one, the years I've spent building companies, leading teams, and solving hard problems, my experience is seen. It's welcomed. People bring me into rooms where things are being shaped. They ask real questions. They're open to new angles. It feels mutual.

At the other, the same experience doesn't always land. It takes more time. Insight doesn't move as easily. Doors don't open in the same way. It's not that anyone's hostile. It's just a different rhythm, built on different defaults. And I don't always fit those.

Early on, I remember asking myself quietly, *How do I lead here without position? How do I contribute when my credibility isn't assumed?*

The answer didn't show up all at once.

What I learned to do first was listen and I started noticing who seemed open. Who paused when I spoke. Who circled back after a meeting. Slowly, a few relationships began to take shape. Not formal partnerships. Just people who were willing to make room for what I brought. Over time, they became bridges. They opened paths I couldn't walk on my own.

It hasn't always worked. I've had setbacks. Long silences. Moments of real discouragement. There have been seasons where I wondered whether it was worth it to stay. But I did stay. And the reason I've stayed is simple: I've kept building credibility.

Not by insisting on being heard. Not by forcing insight into the room.

But by solving real problems. By showing up with care. By holding myself to a standard I would want others to hold, whether or not anyone's watching.

That's what the work of a Loyal Rebel has looked like for me.

I don't carry formal power. I'm not the loudest voice in the room. But I've learned how to recognize the people who are paying attention. I've learned how to help the system see what it hasn't noticed yet.

When the moment feels right, when trust has built and timing lines up, I try to use that influence to ask the next question. To name the next tension. To offer a way forward.

Not to be right.

Not to prove anything.

But because I still believe the mission matters.

PUTTING IT TO WORK

Industry

If you're leading a team, a department, or maybe even a whole organization, there's something worth paying attention to. You probably already have Loyal Rebels around you.

They may not be loud. They may not be the ones people look to first. But they're there. Usually watching carefully. Listening. Trying to make things better in quiet ways, often without being asked, and often without getting much credit.

The question isn't whether they exist. It's whether the space around them allows them to keep going. Whether the system you're in knows how to make room for what they bring. Whether it's smart enough and safe enough for their way of working to take hold.

LOYAL REBELS VS. DISRUPTIVE DISSENTERS

Dimension	Loyal Rebel	Disruptive Dissenter
Intention	Aims to improve outcomes for the team or mission	Aims for control, recognition, or emotional release
Track Record	Known for follow-through and adding value	Known for friction, blame, or unresolved conflict
Timing	Raises issues when they're likely to be heard	Speaks up regardless of readiness or capacity
Alternatives	Offers options or reframes the problem	Fixates on flaws without offering a way forward
Relational Posture	Challenges ideas while protecting relationships	Makes it personal or adversarial
Engagement	Stays involved, even when disagreed with	Disengages or withdraws if not validated

Figure 6: This table distinguishes the "loyal rebel," whose dissent is anchored in shared purpose and constructive partnership, from the "disruptive dissenter," whose challenges erode trust and hinder progress. Use it as a quick lens to evaluate whether push-back in your team is fuel for improvement or friction without forward motion.

LOYAL REBELS VS. DISRUPTIVE DISSENTERS: TELLING CONSTRUCTIVE CHALLENGE FROM CORROSIVE NOISE

Inside any healthy system, challenge is not a threat but a vital sign. Yet dissent can arrive in two very different packages. The loyal rebel pushes from a deep commitment to the mission: they surface blind spots, offer workable options, and stay to help carry the weight of change. Their criticism is rooted in care and reinforced by a track record of follow-through. Timing matters to them; they speak when ears are open and resources are available, amplifying, not splintering collective energy.

The disruptive dissenter may sound similar at first, but their center of gravity is elsewhere. The goal is less about improving the work and more about relieving personal tension, gaining control, or seizing attention. Ideas are challenged without protecting relationships, alternatives are scarce, and conversation becomes a cul-de-sac of blame. Even when a viable path forward is offered, they often disengage, proof that the real target was never progress.

The table highlights six diagnostic dimensions, intention, track record, timing, alternatives, relational posture, and engagement, so leaders can distinguish constructive agitation from corrosive noise. Knowing the difference allows you to amplify voices that strengthen the system while redirecting or containing those that erode trust.

REFLECTION PROMPT

Think of a moment when you challenged a decision that mattered.

Which column did your behavior most resemble?

Scan the six dimensions: where did you show up as a loyal rebel, and where did you drift toward disruptive dissent?

Note one concrete practice you could adopt to deepen your constructive influence next time.

REFLECTION PROMPT FOR LEADERS: TRANSLATING DISSENT INTO MOMENTUM

Take five quiet minutes and answer honestly, without editing, the three questions below.

1. Whose criticism stings but also sticks?
   Name one person whose push-back lingers in your mind after meetings.

2. What signal might be hiding inside their friction?
   List a single concern they raise that, if true, would meaningfully improve the work.

3. What reciprocal next step could you offer?

Write one sentence you will say this week that (a) acknowledges their insight and (b) invites them to help shape a constructive path forward.

Keep the note where you make your next big decision; let it remind you that disciplined dissent is an asset provided you choose to hear it.

That doesn't mean you have to throw everything out and start over. It just means noticing where there's friction, and asking if that friction is telling you something worth learning from.

You can start small.

- Make space for disagreement that doesn't cost someone their footing.
- Pay attention to how people describe the problem, not just how they try to solve it.
- Back the ones who speak up early, even if they don't say it perfectly.

Organizations that stay flexible over time tend to have people like this close to the center when the pressure is high. That's not luck. That's a kind of depth, and it doesn't happen by accident. It can be built, but it works better if you build it before the crisis shows up.

Professional Career

If you're leading from the middle or even just trying to, some of this might feel familiar. You may already be moving in the Loyal Rebel direction, or at least thinking about it. But this part comes with a bit of a caution.

Don't rush into that role too fast if you haven't laid the groundwork because most systems are slower to trust challenges that don't come with context.

When trust hasn't been built, even a useful critique can land sideways. People might not hear it as care. They might hear it as conflict. Or as over-reach. Or just as disruption that's hard to place.

That doesn't mean you should stay quiet. It just means the order of things matters.

Before you challenge:

- Show up in ways people can rely on.
- Focus on the problems that already matter to others, not just the ones that frustrate you.
- Learn how the system sees itself, so you can speak in a way that makes sense inside it.

Let people feel your steadiness before they encounter your resistance. Let them see your care before they hear your critique. That's what helps your voice land in a way that others can hold.

Personal Life

This is about how you move through your life. Your communities, your family, your friendships, your team. Anywhere people gather and try to move together, the same questions show up. The same tensions. The same patterns.

And maybe just as importantly, the same quiet practices that help you stay grounded while things shift.

- Speak in ways that leave the relationship intact.
- Tie your insight to something shared, so it doesn't get dismissed as just personal frustration.
- Pay attention to your capacity, especially if you're the one holding the edge.

You don't need permission to lead. And you don't need a title. But you do need something steadier underneath. A kind of center you can return to when the room gets loud or when the ground gets shaky.

Build that first, and keep tending to it.

7

THE POWER OF STARTING WITH WHAT YOU HAVE

The leaders I admire most are the ones who stay grounded. When things get shaky, they tend to have something in common. They don't wait around for the conditions to be perfect. They don't hold their breath until everything lines up just right. They move when it feels just real enough to try.

In the world of entrepreneurship, there's a term for this kind of thinking. It's called effectual logic. But I don't think you need to be steeped in theory to recognize it. It's less about having a plan and more about being willing to begin. The focus isn't on predicting exactly where you'll end up. It's more about working with what's in front of you and seeing what's possible from there.

It's not that these leaders don't have a vision. They do. It's just that they don't treat certainty as a requirement for progress. They're not outsourcing action to some future moment when everything makes sense.

That kind of thinking can be hard to recognize in organizations where there's a strong pull toward planning. Most companies are built to scale, so they lean on what's often called causal logic. You set a goal, build a plan to get there, and then you follow the plan. That works well when things are steady and when the environment isn't moving too fast.

But a lot of the time, things aren't steady. Markets shift. Budgets shrink. The ask grows faster than the team can keep up. When that happens, the old models start to creak. Leaders find themselves needing something else. Another way to move.

That's where "effectual leadership" comes in.

Effectual leaders don't pretend the uncertainty isn't there. They don't wait for it to go away. They work with it. They look at what they already have the skills, relationships, time, credibility, and even just the willingness to try, and they start from there. Then they learn as they go. They adjust without giving up.

Years ago, this approach was formally described in the field of entrepreneurship as "effectuation," a decision-making logic rooted in how expert founders actually operate when the path ahead is uncertain. Instead of starting with prediction, they begin with the means at hand and allow action, interaction, and adjustment to shape what becomes possible. I've found this same approach deeply relevant in leadership, especially inside systems that don't sit still.

Effectuation is built around five core principles that describe how progress happens when prediction doesn't hold. While the original research was rooted in entrepreneurship, I've seen these same patterns show up in all kinds of leadership, especially when things are changing quickly or when the way forward isn't obvious. What follows is my interpretation of those principles, not as theory to memorize, but as ways of noticing what we might already be doing and how to do it with more intention.

START WITH WHAT YOU HAVE

It starts with a simple question: What do you already have? Who are you? What do you know? Who do you know?

Effectual leaders like the ones I've seen in practice don't wait for permission or for the stars to align. They don't hold off until they get the right funding or the perfect team. They look at what's within reach. What's already in their grasp. They begin with that; even if it's not enough to finish the job, it's usually enough to start.

Know What You Can Risk

Instead of asking, "What's the return?" they ask, "What can I afford to lose?" That shift matters. It helps leaders make decisions when the stakes feel high or the path is unclear.

This doesn't mean they're reckless. It means they're practical. They define the downside up front so when they move, they're not guessing. They've already decided they can live with the risk, and they do this even when the outcome is unclear. That makes experimentation possible and lowers the emotional cost of learning as you go.

Build Together As You Go

This one is about people. About how collaboration happens in real life, not just on paper.

Effectual leaders don't wait to find people who agree with every part of their vision. They look for those who are willing to build something together. Especially in the early stages when the work is messy and the path isn't clear, they lean into the relationships where co-creation is possible. Where people are willing to commit, even if the end goal hasn't been fully defined yet. That kind of partnership changes the shape of the work itself.

Let Surprises Shape The Work

Surprises happen. Plans fall through. What you expected doesn't always show up.

Where some leaders see that as a problem to fix, effectual leaders treat it as part of the process. When something unexpected shows up, they pause and ask, "What else could this be?"

The shift from resistance to curiosity opens up new directions. It doesn't mean you love every surprise. But it does mean you're willing to look at what's there and see if something new can come from it.

Lead From What You Can Control

This one goes to the heart of what makes this kind of leadership work. It's the idea that the future isn't something you wait for because it's something you shape, starting with what you can control.

You don't need to predict everything. You just need to keep moving from where you are. That kind of agency gives you the sense that what you do matters, even if the picture isn't complete. It's what keeps leaders going when the rest of the system feels uncertain.

Most of the leaders I spend time with are already working this way. They might not name it as a specific method, but the behavior is there: steady, adaptive, and real.

They're in meetings, trying to stretch a budget that won't quite cover what's needed. Or they're listening closely, hoping to catch a moment of clarity in the middle of too many moving parts. They're calling in favors, leaning on someone's insight, nudging a project forward even when the full strategy hasn't landed yet.

They're doing it without a clear roadmap. Without a guarantee. With partial data and only scattered alignment, and with no one often naming what they're doing as leadership, it doesn't follow the usual pattern.

They imagine that somewhere out there, the real leaders have more certainty. Or more permission. Or more control. But in my experience, that's not usually true. What's true is that these leaders are already doing the hard part. They're moving through complexity without waiting for it to clear up.

What they need next isn't a perfect plan. They don't need more steps or better answers. What they need is something that makes sense of what they're already doing. A way to name it. To steady it. To trust it more fully. And to keep going when it still feels a little murky.

That's where this kind of cycle becomes useful. Not as a new framework to follow, but as a kind of mirror. It's something that reflects what's already happening and helps strengthen it. It doesn't replace instinct. It gives shape to it and opens up a path forward, even when the full destination isn't clear yet.

Effectual leadership isn't just a way of thinking. It's also a way of moving. It's a process that loops, adapts, and stays grounded in what's real. It reflects a pattern of decision-making that emerges when the future isn't clear. One that helps leaders stay in motion, even when they don't know exactly what's coming next.

It's different from most of the strategy models you'll find in organizations. Those tend to move in a straight line: define the goal, make the plan, execute the plan.

But this kind of process doesn't work like that. It turns. It loops. It shifts shape as you move through it.

You begin with what you have. Then you start to interact with others. You make small commitments. You build together. Somewhere in the middle of that, the opportunity starts to shift because the act of engaging has changed what's possible.

Then, almost without realizing, it begins again. You've got new tools now. Maybe more clarity. Maybe new people. And so the cycle starts over, but it's not the same cycle. It's wider this time. Maybe deeper. Maybe slower or faster depending on what's changed.

IT STARTS WITH WHAT YOU ALREADY HAVE

This process always begins in the same place. With means.

When we say *means*, we're not just talking about resources in the usual sense. It's a broader idea. It's who you are. What you know. Who you know. It's what you carry with you. It's your perspective, your lived experience, the values you fall back on when things get uncertain. It's the relationships you've built over time, especially the ones rooted in real trust.

There's another way to think about it, one that helps bring it into focus, especially inside organizations. *Means* are your core competencies. They're the things you or your team or your company are especially good at. The capacities you've built, the kinds of problems you're equipped to solve, and the specific ways you create value in the world.

Leaders begin there, not because it's everything they'll need, and not because they know exactly where it will lead, but because it gives them something solid to move from. It gives them footing.

Understanding those core competencies matters. More than just at a surface level, but with real clarity because without that understanding, it's hard to see the shape of what's possible. It's hard to know what kinds of problems you're actually ready to take on. In the kind of work we've talked about, where opportunity isn't handed to you fully formed, but shaped over time, that clarity becomes essential.

Earlier, we spent time on the relationship between problems, solutions, and the business models that support them. We discussed how opportunity isn't just found, it's built.

But you can't build something meaningful if you don't know what tools are in your hands. Or where your strengths lie. Or how your team's skills fit together in practice. So this step of reflection on means is not a pause before the real work begins. It is the beginning of the work. Can you articulate your core competencies? Those of your team? Your company?

And it's not abstract. Not if you really look. In complex, fast-moving environments, waiting for full clarity can turn into paralysis. But starting from what's already present, starting from the ground you're standing on, that's how momentum builds. That's how new possibilities begin to show up: it's because you're moving, and motion creates its own kind of visibility, even when the path forward isn't clear.

COLLABORATION THAT CHANGES THE WORK

Once you begin moving from your means, that is once you've taken that first step based on what's already in your hands, then you begin to reach out. And that's when other people begin to show up.

This part is about interaction, but not the kind that's just about updates or alignment. It's not about managing stakeholders in the usual sense. It's about co-creating something that wasn't there before and allowing others to bring their own means, their own competencies, constraints, experiences, and values, and letting those reshape the opportunity.

The phrase "crazy quilt" captures it well. It's messy, patchwork, improvised. You bring your piece. Someone else brings theirs. Slowly, something bigger and more useful takes shape, driven not by one person's directive, but by shared engagement.

This is where things really start to move. When someone joins, not just to advise, but to commit, you get more than help. You get access to their perspective. Their resources. Their constraints. Their sense of what matters.

Those contributions don't just add to the work. They reshape it. They shift the contours of the opportunity. They help clarify what kind of problem you're solving and how the solution might take form in a way that fits the moment. Especially if you're building on top of what you and your team already do well, this process helps stretch and sharpen where those competencies meet real-world needs.

Each time someone makes a commitment, it lowers uncertainty just a little and in the way that says, "This isn't just an idea anymore. We're in this now." That commitment creates a kind of anchor because it brings weight and shape to what was only a possibility a moment ago, and it does so without any guarantee of success.

It's easy to miss how significant this is. When you're in the middle of it, it can feel like small conversations, loose threads, tiny bets. This is how real progress begins: with shared action, not certainty, by building something others want to be part of, not by convincing everyone up front.

If you're paying attention, these moments of engagement will teach you more about your own means. They reveal how your competencies interact with others'. Where they hold, where they stretch, and where they might need to evolve. You begin to see more clearly what kinds of problems you can keep solving and which ones might not be yours to carry.

That's the ongoing work. It doesn't finish with a neat decision. It opens the door to the next version of what this opportunity might become.

SHAPING THE GOAL AS YOU GO

In more traditional, causal models, the goal is where you start. You define it early. You point everything toward it. That's the structure most of us are taught to expect. Figure out where you're headed and then build the plan to get there.

But that's not always how real work unfolds. Especially not in complex systems and not when you're trying to do something new, or when the terrain keeps shifting under your feet.

Effectual leadership works differently. The goal isn't fixed at the beginning, it's shaped as you go. It changes in response to the people who join, the insights that emerge, the constraints you run into, and the things you try that don't work. All of that is part of the process. It's not a detour. It's the path itself.

That starts as a loosely defined direction, more of a hunch than a plan, becomes more grounded by letting it be shaped by others rather than trying to refine it solely in your own mind. When people commit, when they bring their means into the mix, their needs and goals become part of the fabric, and the opportunity becomes something co-authored.

This isn't about giving up control. It's about letting the work get smarter. Letting it reflect more of the system it lives in. In that process, you begin to see which of your competencies are most valuable to the shared effort and which ones might need to be set aside for now.

That's part of the leadership work: knowing your strengths and being open to the opportunity to evolve based on where the energy and alignment actually are. That takes some trust. It takes letting go of the idea that leadership means having the full picture from the start.

The opportunity itself isn't discovered like treasure. It's shaped like clay. Pressed into form through action, relationship, timing, and tension. And just like clay, it responds to pressure. It holds some shapes better than others. You learn that by working with it.

Something else happens as that shape starts to emerge. You, the person leading, begin to shift too. Because you're not standing outside the process. You're in it. You're being shaped right alongside the work.

Each cycle, each interaction, each moment of commitment teaches you something about the opportunity, and equally about yourself: how you lead, what you need, and where growth is happening.

It's not just the opportunity that gets co-constructed. The leader does, too.

WHAT YOU BUILD OVER TIME

As you move through this cycle again and again, something begins to shift. Not always in ways that are easy to name. But if you pause and look back, you'll notice that the work and you aren't quite where you started.

Each round through the process gives you more to work with. More people, more insight, more experience. The core competencies that you began with, those skills, instincts, and relationships that made the first move possible, start to expand. They get tested and refined. Some get sharper. Others shift altogether. And sometimes, you find new ones you didn't realize were there.

This repetition isn't just about practice. It's about transformation. With each cycle, your resource base grows quietly and meaningfully: a new collaborator, a clearer understanding of what your team can deliver under pressure, and a mental model that helps you navigate a tricky decision with more steadiness than before.

THE MORAL DRIFT MAP

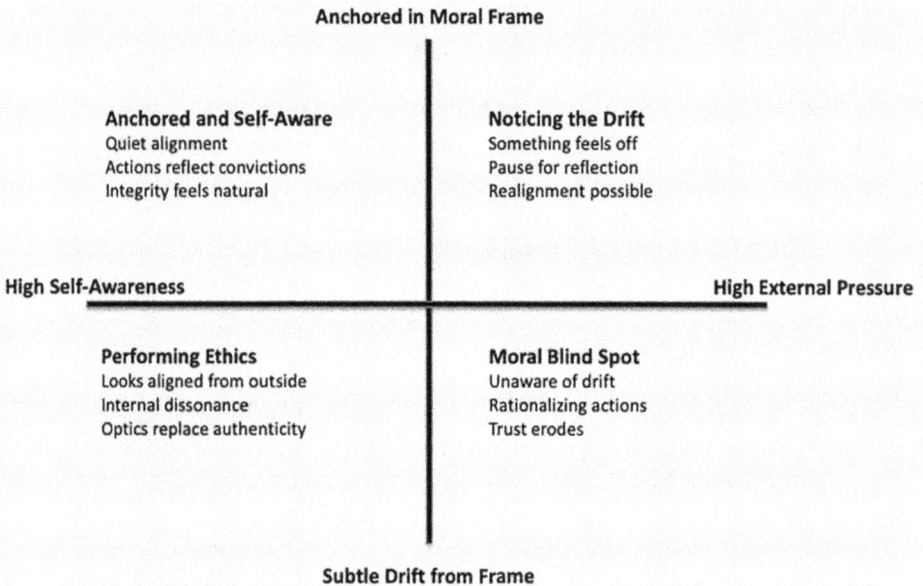

Anchored in Moral Frame

Anchored and Self-Aware
Quiet alignment
Actions reflect convictions
Integrity feels natural

Noticing the Drift
Something feels off
Pause for reflection
Realignment possible

High Self-Awareness

High External Pressure

Performing Ethics
Looks aligned from outside
Internal dissonance
Optics replace authenticity

Moral Blind Spot
Unaware of drift
Rationalizing actions
Trust erodes

Subtle Drift from Frame

Figure 7: This four-quadrant "Moral Drift Map" shows how the cross-pressures of self-awareness and external demands shape a leader's ethical stance—from quietly aligned, to drifting, to outright blind spots. Use it as a quick mirror to notice where you stand, then course-correct before subtle compromises harden into habits.

INTERPRETING THE MAP:
LEADING FROM YOUR INNER FRAME

Leaders don't lose their ethical compass in a single moment—it drifts. And often, the drift is subtle. The Moral Drift Map captures this process, not as a judgment tool, but as a self-awareness guide. It offers four zones of moral alignment, each shaped by a leader's internal clarity and the pressure of the external environment.

In the top-left quadrant, leaders are Anchored and Self-Aware. There is no dissonance between action and value, no hidden cost behind the scenes. Integrity here is lived, not performed. In contrast, the Performing Ethics zone in the bottom-left reflects high awareness but compromised authenticity. Leaders here know something is off, but perform alignment for optics or survival.

On the right side of the map, external pressure becomes the dominant force. In the Noticing the Drift zone, leaders feel the misalignment, but still have a window for reflection and realignment. The most dangerous quadrant— Moral Blind Spot—is when drift becomes invisible. Actions are rationalized. Justifications multiply. And over time, trust begins to erode.

The map is a mirror. It invites you not to label others, but to ask yourself: Where am I standing? What's shaping my decisions today? And how do I return to my inner frame?

REFLECTION PROMPT

Think back to a time when you felt pressure to act in a way that didn't fully align with your values.

- Where on the Moral Drift Map would you place yourself in that moment?

- What signals—internal or external—did you notice, ignore, or rationalize?

- What might you do differently now to stay closer to your inner frame?

Alongside that, your ability to notice patterns gets stronger. You start to recognize when an opportunity is worth leaning into. When a signal is real, and when it's just noise. You learn to read systems more clearly because *you've lived through them,* and when that happens, uncertainty becomes less daunting.

Your credibility grows in a steady, earned way. People begin to trust that when you say something will move, it probably will because you've shown that you can act, adapt, and keep going.

Something quieter happens as well. Your relationship with ambiguity changes. It's still there. It still tugs at you. But it's not as paralyzing. You've seen that motion is possible even when the outcome isn't guaranteed. You've learned that action doesn't always require certainty.

Over time, that builds a kind of calm. Not because things get easier, but because you've gotten more fluent inside the difficulty.

That fluency isn't just strategic, it's emotional. It helps you stay grounded when the way forward isn't obvious. It lets you be honest with your team when things are murky, without losing momentum. It gives you the range to lead through complexity without needing to pretend that everything's clear.

All of this, the growing competencies, the deeper instincts, and the quiet confidence, becomes part of how you engage the next cycle. You carry those learnings with you. You enter with a little more steadiness and maybe a little more humility, too. If the process teaches anything, it's that certainty is temporary and learning is ongoing.

So each time you begin again, you do it with more texture. More depth and with a lived sense of how the process works. Of your role inside it and how your leadership is being shaped, not outside the work, but inside it.

This makes effectual leadership particularly powerful inside organizations undergoing change. When conditions are shifting too fast for predictive planning to keep up, the "effectual cycle" offers an alternative: *decide, engage, adjust, repeat.*

HOW LEADERSHIP CHANGES THROUGH THE CYCLE

As this process repeats with each iteration being a little different, each time shaped by new people and new conditions, you start to notice certain shifts in how you think and how you lead. They're not things you decide all at once. They emerge over time. They come from trying, adjusting, watching what works, and sitting with what doesn't.

Slowly, certain behaviors begin to take root, not because you adopted a new leadership style, but because the work asked for it and you responded.

From Control to Collaboration

One of the first shifts is around control. Early on, it can feel like your job is to hold everything together. To steer. To keep things on track.

But over time, you start to see that progress doesn't come from holding tight as much as it comes from opening up and inviting others to help shape the direction and take ownership.

That kind of shared ownership changes things. It makes the work more durable because now it doesn't rely entirely on your clarity or capacity. It's being carried by more than one person, which creates space for the opportunity to grow in ways you couldn't have made happen alone.

From Precision to Iteration

The second shift has to do with how you move forward. Early on, you might feel pressure to get it right and be precise, plan thoroughly, and anticipate every outcome. But as you go, you start to realize that the early steps don't have to be exact. They just have to be honest. And real.

What matters is that you're moving with intention, even if the full picture isn't clear yet. Once you're in motion, you can see more. You can adjust. The clarity you were waiting for will come through action, not before it.

From Risk Avoidance to Affordable Loss

Then there's the shift in how you think about risk. In the beginning, it's easy to fixate on what could go wrong. To try to build plans that avoid failure altogether. But effectual leadership asks a different question. What can I afford to lose?

That question doesn't make risk disappear, but it makes it manageable. It gives you a way to take small bets and try something before it's fully proven. To learn from what doesn't work without losing the thread.

These shifts aren't rules. They're more like postures, ways of being in the work that help you stay with it. Ways of leading that don't rely on perfection, but on presence. On showing up, again and again, and finding a way forward with the tools you've got.

CONSTRAINTS ARE THE CANVAS

If means are where you start, think of it like the ground under your feet, then constraints are the edges. The frame. They shape what's possible, and they also shape what's needed.

It can be easy to see constraints as something in the way. As friction. In a lot of organizations, they feel like that. Limited budget. Layers of approval. Systems that weren't built for change. Culture that leans cautious. The list is usually long. If you're trying to move something forward, those limits can feel like a weight.

But over time, effectual leaders start to see them differently, not as blockers, but as the structure you get to work within. A kind of creative tension. Something that narrows the field just enough to help you focus. When everything feels possible, it's hard to know where to begin. But when certain paths are closed, others come into sharper view.

Constraints, in that way, aren't the opposite of innovation. They're the conditions that make innovation take shape.

This matters, especially when you're leading inside an existing system. Those constraints, whether they're financial, structural, or cultural, are part of the landscape. They don't go away just because you've got a good idea.

So instead of resisting them, effectual leaders work with them. They treat them as inputs. They learn what the system can tolerate. Where there's give. Where there isn't. And what that means for how they lead.

That kind of fluency doesn't show up in a single moment. It's built cycle by cycle. Each time you engage, you learn something more about the problem you're trying to solve and the system around it. How to match your team's core competencies to the real constraints on the ground. How to stretch without snapping. How to make something new without getting shut down.

Sometimes, the constraint itself reveals the opportunity. A regulation closes one path, and you're forced to think more carefully. A staffing gap forces the team to simplify. A limitation in one place surfaces unexpected capacity somewhere else. That tension, between what you want to do and what's actually possible, is often where the best work begins to take shape.

Effective leaders don't try to erase those limits. They learn to see them more clearly, shape within them, and eventually build the credibility that lets them test the edges a little further. Progress emerges through steady proof, bit-by-bit, that the system can hold more than it once believed.

That's a kind of intelligence that doesn't always look like strategy in the formal sense, but it's just as important. Maybe more so. Because it's the difference between a leader who can imagine change and one who can navigate it.

Within this process, surprises are not a flaw. They're part of the material. Contingency is expected. The appearance of the unexpected in the form of new data, new resistance, and new energy is not a problem to avoid. It's a signal. Something to respond to. Something to work with.

So the goal is not to eliminate disruption. It's to build enough flexibility that you can let disruption change the direction, without derailing the whole effort.

That's what effective leadership makes room for: movement within limits, progress without guarantees, and a kind of creativity that grows because the constraints become a catalyst, not a roadblock.

In corporate environments, especially the ones built for scale, this way of leading becomes *essential* as well as useful. These are systems that move slowly in some ways and fast in others. They carry weight. They carry history. And they weren't always designed for adaptability.

Learning how to lead inside those limits, but without letting the limits shrink your leadership, is its own kind of practice. It asks something of you. It asks for patience, resilience, and a willingness to keep learning in real time.

Effectual leaders don't wait for the conditions to get easier. They learn to move through what's already here. To keep shaping, listening, adjusting. To stay with the process even when it's uncertain. Especially when it's uncertain.

Because the goal isn't control, and it isn't perfection. It's the ability to stay in motion and let the work keep unfolding without needing to know exactly how it will end.

A LIFE LIVED:

Finding Footing After the Fall

People sometimes ask how I ended up becoming a professor after running my own business for years. I understand the curiosity. It doesn't look like the usual path when you lay it out. I didn't follow an academic track. I didn't map out a future that pointed to teaching.

But when I look back now, I can trace the steps. I just didn't have the language for it then. I didn't know what to call it.

What I now know is called the effectual cycle was just how I, and most entrepreneurs, operated. I didn't think of it as a framework. I didn't know there was a name for it. I just did what made sense to me. I looked at the situation and tried to figure out where I might be useful. I thought about what I knew that students might not, and then I looked at what I had to work with.

At that point, what I had wasn't credentials in the academic sense. I didn't have research or publications, but I had time in the field. Years of building things. Trying things. Leading teams through uncertainty. Learning how to make hard calls without knowing everything. Learning how to take a hit and get back up. That was the toolkit I was holding. I didn't earn it in a classroom, but it was real, and it was mine.

What people usually don't see is the timing of it all. The invitation to teach didn't come when things were going well. It showed up during one of the hardest stretches I've ever known. I had just closed my business, and it wasn't a clean ending. It was heavy. Financially. Emotionally. Personally. I lost a lot. I carried a sense of failure that went deeper than I could have imagined. It felt like something permanent had come to an end.

And still something moved. Something in me kept going. I've noticed this pattern. Some of the hardest moments I've lived through were followed by something surprising. It wasn't because everything turned around all at once, it was because I didn't stop. I kept moving. Even when I couldn't see where it was heading, I stayed in motion. I worked with what I had. And what I had then was experience. A voice. And a kind of quiet willingness to share what I'd learned. Especially the parts that were earned the hard way.

So I said yes. The first chance that came along, I took it; I saw a need and knew I could help. I didn't wait until it all felt clear. I didn't ask for a sign. I started with what I had. Then I figured the next part out. That first class opened a door, and one student conversation led to another. It wouldn't have made sense on paper, and it wasn't part of some strategy.

One project opened up a path I hadn't seen before. It wasn't a leap forward. It didn't feel like progress in the traditional sense. It was more like stepping onto a rock in a stream, just stable enough to stand on, just close enough to reach from where I was. Then I saw the next one. And the next. The movement wasn't planned out in advance. It was about finding footing as I went.

Later, I saw what I had been doing. I had been making space for opportunity. Creating it, really. The pattern wasn't complicated. It looked like this: there was a problem. I had an idea for how to respond, and there was a way to make it work. That was the shape of it.

The problem was simple in that too many students were learning business in ways that felt disconnected from what the work actually felt like. The solution was to bring real experience into the room. A lived life, supported by academic research.

In those early days, the model was just me. My time. My voice. My willingness to be honest about what I'd been through.

It didn't feel polished. It didn't feel impressive. But it felt real, and it moved things forward. That's the part I've come to trust most. When things fall apart, sometimes the next thing you build isn't a fix. It's something you couldn't have seen before. It's something new that only becomes visible on the other side of the loss.

Each time I stood in front of a classroom, I noticed I had a little more to bring. More pattern recognition. More openness. More capacity to sit with not knowing. I was still doing what I had always done; I was working with what was available. I was saying yes to what came. I was staying open to what might take shape.

Effectual thinking didn't change how I moved through the world. It gave me a way to describe what had always felt true. Not all strategy begins with a destination. Sometimes, it begins with a question. Or with a conversation. Or with the simple act of stepping into a room and asking, quietly, "Where can I be useful?"

PUTTING IT TO WORK: THREE DIMENSIONS OF APPLICATION

Industry

Effectual thinking isn't just an abstract theory. It's a practical way of leading when things are uncertain and the usual plans don't quite work. In the world of business, this means taking action with what you have in front of you, with the knowledge you already carry, with the people you already trust, and with the resources you can actually access. It's about starting now, not waiting for a perfect forecast or for everything to line up neatly.

Some of the ventures that ended up being the most successful started with a lot of unknowns, incomplete information, and a quiet decision to go ahead anyway. What makes the difference isn't being able to predict the future. It's about being able to adjust, to adapt as things unfold. A team that knows how to keep moving, learning, and adjusting will always have an edge over one that's waiting for certainty because certainty might never arrive.

Professional Career

When it comes to your career, the next opportunity you're looking for probably isn't going to show up on a job board. It's likely already beginning in a conversation, in some kind of collaboration, in a pattern you've started to notice. Effectual thinking offers a different lens on career-building.

Rather than asking yourself, *Where do I want to be in five years?* it asks, *What can I do right now, with what I already know, who I already know, and what I already care about?*

The effectual cycle lets you act even when you don't have the full picture. It lets you try things without needing to explain every move or have a detailed blueprint. It teaches you to see each step as part of something larger that's being built, even if that something doesn't look clear yet. Even the missteps matter because they're all part of the foundation you're creating.

Personal Life

In life, much like in leadership, we rarely have the full story. Effectual thinking can be a compass when things feel unclear. It encourages you to start with what you already have in hand, your values, your skills, and the relationships you've built, and to trust that moving forward, even in small ways, is more important than waiting for everything to be just right.

Whether you're making a decision about a big move, a family choice, or just navigating a period of uncertainty, this mindset helps you reframe the unknown. It's not something to be afraid of, it's an opening, an invitation.

Sometimes, the moments that end up defining our lives don't start with grand plans or perfect timing. They start with small steps, sometimes unfinished or imperfect. The key is to keep moving. To stay present. To listen. And to trust that what's coming next will take shape as you move through it, not because of it.

8

LEADING WITH A MORAL COMPASS

M ost organizations don't lack rules. There are plenty of policies and protocols. Legal documents. Compliance checklists. All the structures that are supposed to guide behavior and protect against risk. A lot of the time, they help. But not always. Not when you end up in the in-between places.

That space where the right answer isn't clear. Where it isn't about what's legal or even what's allowed. It's about something else. Something that feels heavier, because it carries more weight. That's where the rules stop being enough and the moral compass comes in.

I don't mean a slogan on the wall or a code of conduct. I don't mean branding. I mean something internal. Quiet. Like a sense of direction when there's no map. It doesn't make decisions easier, but it can make them more honest. More grounded. And over time, more consistent.

If you've been in leadership for any amount of time, especially in complex environments like ones with competing goals, shifting conditions, or different cultures or values, you already know that technical skill and authority only take you so far. The rest depends on something else.

Integrity that stays with you. Not stubborn or rigid, but steady. Something that helps you stay yourself in the middle of change.

Leading with a moral compass doesn't mean you're always right. That's not the point. It's more about knowing where you are and where you won't go. And being able to act from that place, even when it's hard. Even when there's a cost.

I won't tell you where those lines should be. That's not what this is. Honestly, I don't think that's a leader's job anyway. But I do think it matters that you've done that work for yourself. That you know what matters to you. That you've thought through where your lines are and why they're there.

Because these days, people are watching. There's more visibility than ever. More pressure. More expectation. If you're leading without a moral compass, you're not just unmoored, you may actually be a risk to others.

But if you have one and you've learned to listen to it, you become something else. Someone people can count on. Someone who stays centered. Someone who doesn't shake loose when the pressure builds.

WHAT A MORAL COMPASS ACTUALLY DOES

A moral compass won't solve complexity. That's not what it's for. It's more like a guide you carry with you while you move through it.

It won't protect you from hard calls or make conflict disappear, but it does help you stay oriented when the path is messy. When all your choices feel compromised. When your instincts and your incentives are pulling in different directions.

If you use it well, your moral compass helps in a few specific ways.

A moral compass gives you a filter. When you're staring at choices that all look equally valid or equally flawed, it helps you remove the ones that don't fit with what you believe.

A moral compass helps build trust. Not just with your team or your customers. With yourself.

A moral compass helps you stay steady across different situations. The setting can change. The stakes can rise. But your compass stays with you.

It won't always be obvious or easy. But if you've spent time with it and you've learned to check it, you'll show up with more consistency. And the people around you will feel that.

You'll see it in things like:

- Saying no to a client, even when the numbers say yes.
- Letting someone go in a way that honors their dignity.
- Taking the blame when that's what's right.
- Protecting your values, even when it costs something.

In those moments, you might ask yourself, *What am I really optimizing for here? Does it reflect who I want to be?*

Sometimes, just asking that question is enough to change what happens next.

THE SPACE BETWEEN

Before we talk more about boundaries and where they fit, it helps to sit for a moment with the space in between. The tension. The quiet tug that happens when something doesn't feel quite right, even if you can't explain exactly why.

Almost every leader I know has had a moment like that. Maybe they were walking out of a meeting. Maybe they were at home, late at night, turning something over in their mind. Sometimes it's a conversation that lingers. Sometimes it's a decision that didn't feel quite clean. And they find themselves wondering, *Is this still okay?*

Sometimes, the answer is clear. The discomfort shows up immediately. But other times, it takes longer. It settles in more slowly. You start by brushing it off, telling yourself it's not a big deal. Everyone else seems fine with it. Maybe you're overthinking it. But that unsettled feeling stays with you.

The truth is, the hardest moments in leadership aren't always the ones that are clearly wrong. They're not big, bold violations. They're not obvious breaches. They're more subtle than that. They're the moments that are almost wrong. Just off enough to notice, but not enough to sound the alarm.

They're the things that are easy to justify. The trade-offs that seem small. The decisions that feel necessary, even when they don't sit right. Things that, on the surface, look normal. But somewhere underneath, you feel a shift, like a small step in the wrong direction.

That's where the compass gets tested, in the quiet moments. The ambiguous ones. That's also where boundaries start to matter because they give you something firm to hold onto when the ground starts to slide.

MORAL COMPASS VS. ETHICAL BOUNDARIES

Things rarely fall apart in a single moment. Cultures erode slowly through little things. The small jokes no one calls out. The numbers no one questions. The choices no one owns.

Over time, what felt like a sharp edge starts to blur. People stop noticing just how far they've drifted.

That's why boundaries matter. You have to name them. You have to protect them. You have to model them before the pressure comes. Once things start moving fast, it's too late to find your footing.

A moral compass is internal. It's personal. It's shaped by your beliefs and your sense of integrity. Boundaries are more visible. They're the edges of that compass. The places you've decided you won't cross.

Think of the compass as your orientation system. It helps you pick a direction. It might evolve over time, but it stays rooted in what matters most to you. It influences how you show up, how you decide, and what you notice.

Boundaries are the lines. They're not as flexible. They don't adjust to context. They're the stops that keep you from sliding too far, and they bring clarity to others, too. When people know where you stand, they feel more secure. More able to speak up. More willing to trust.

But here's something important: boundaries without a compass can harden into dogma, and a compass without boundaries can be used to rationalize almost anything.

You need both.

The compass helps you move. The boundaries help you hold.

Together, they shape how you lead when no one's looking.

MORAL COMPASS: ORIENTATION

When I talk about a moral compass, I don't mean something rigid or lofty. I mean the deeper kind of orientation. The sense of direction that doesn't just live in your head, but in your gut and your experience and your sense of what matters most. It's what you lean on when the outside signals get fuzzy or when they go silent altogether.

Your moral compass isn't something you pull out only during the big, dramatic decisions. It shows up in the small, daily ones too. In how you listen. In what you notice. In the kinds of trade-offs you're willing to make, and the ones you're not. It influences how you talk to your team and how you respond when things go wrong. How you hold power, even when no one's looking.

It's not fixed like a rulebook. It can evolve. It deepens with experience. Sometimes it even shifts a little, as your understanding grows. But the core, the part that reflects your convictions, tends to hold steady. That's what helps you navigate, even when everything around you is moving.

When people experience that steadiness, they notice. They learn to trust it. According to a study by Deloitte, over ninety percent of employees say they're more engaged when their leaders show consistent values, even under pressure. It makes sense. We all want to know what kind of person we're following, especially when things get hard.

So your moral compass is more than a feeling. It's more than an idea. It's the way you stay oriented when the path disappears. The more clearly you understand it, the more confidently you can move through uncertainty.

ETHICAL BOUNDARIES: DEFINITION

Ethical boundaries are different. They are more like the outer edges. The places you mark clearly so you don't cross them by accident. They show you what's acceptable and what's not. Not just legally, but personally. In your work. In the culture you're helping to shape.

They don't shift easily. At least they shouldn't because that's part of what gives them strength. These are the hard stops. The outer limits. The guardrails that keep things from slipping slowly into something else.

A global study was released by EY in 2022. It found that forty-two percent of employees felt pressure to compromise their standards. That number is already unsettling. But the part that stayed with me was the next one. Almost a quarter of them said they had actually gone through with it. They had done something they believed was wrong because of the culture around them.

That's what boundaries are there to protect against. Not just for you, but for the people who work with you. When you're clear about where your lines are, others don't have to guess. That clarity makes it easier for them to speak up. To trust. To feel safe in their choices.

When leaders hold and model strong boundaries, the ripple effects are real. Less confusion. Less fear. Less silence. And more room for the kind of trust that holds up under pressure.

But there's something else I've learned, and it feels important to say. Boundaries on their own can go too far. They can get rigid. They can become rules without context, which can lead to judgment. Or shame. Or an unwillingness to adapt when the situation really calls for it.

On the other side, a moral compass without boundaries is slippery. It can be used to explain anything. To make exceptions that quietly bend back on themselves. Over time, that flexibility turns into drift.

So the real work is holding both. Knowing how to stay open and steady. Knowing how to move with integrity but still draw the line.

I've come to see it like this. The compass is what helps me move through complexity. It helps me stay pointed in the right direction. But the boundaries are the moat. They protect what matters. They give me just enough structure to resist the things that might wear me down or pull me off course.

It's not about being strong all the time or about resisting everything. It's more about having the right kind of scaffolding. The kind that helps you stay yourself when the pressure shows up.

WHY IT PAYS TO LEAD WITH A MORAL COMPASS

For Organizations

There's a growing body of evidence that organizations led by people with a strong moral compass perform better over time. It's not just a theory. The data keeps showing up in different places.

According to research from Ethisphere, companies that are known for integrity and ethical leadership outperform the S&P 500 by somewhere between seven and ten percent each year.

The reason isn't mysterious. Trust creates stability. Stability makes it easier to do good work. When a company has ethical leadership at the top, there's usually less internal noise. People feel safer. They're not spending energy watching their backs or second-guessing intentions. Turnover is lower. Communication is cleaner. Things move with less friction.

These outcomes might sound like a nice-to-have, but they turn out to be real drivers of performance. Studies from places like Deloitte, Harvard Business School, and Edelman keep showing the same thing. When leaders are consistent in their values and act with clarity and integrity, the people around them trust more. And when trust is high, everything else moves better. Especially when things are uncertain or hard.

When people know what the company stands for, and they see leaders living those values in real time, something shifts. They stop burning energy on politics. They stop guessing what matters. And they start leaning in with more focus and confidence.

Cultures like that aren't just more productive. They're also sturdier. They hold together when things go wrong. They recover more quickly after setbacks. They're less likely to rot quietly from the inside out.

For Individuals

The same patterns show up at the personal level. Research from the *Journal of Applied Psychology* found something simple but important. People who lead from a strong moral identity, meaning they try to stay true to what they believe, are more likely to get promoted, especially in times when things feel uncertain or volatile.

That makes sense. When people around you can count on your steadiness, your clarity, and your ability to stay grounded under pressure, you become an anchor: someone they can rely on when everything else starts to drift and feels uncertain.

There's also a quieter benefit. Leaders who hold to their values tend to experience less burnout. That was shown in a 2015 study in the journal *Organizational Behavior and Human Decision Processes*. They reported lower "cognitive dissonance," which basically means they weren't in constant internal conflict. They also reported feeling more satisfied in their work.

That kind of alignment doesn't just protect your energy. It makes you more centered, and that groundedness tends to show up in every room you walk into.

Trust, it turns out, isn't just about relationships. It's not only about how others see you. It's something that amplifies performance too. The foundation for that trust, the kind that lasts, is moral clarity.

WHEN OTHERS DON'T CARRY A COMPASS

It's one thing to lead with a moral compass. But sometimes you find your-self working with people who don't. Or competing against them. And that brings a different kind of pressure.

When someone in a position of influence starts bending the rules or working in their own interest at the expense of others, it can create a ripple effect. The whole system around them feels it. There's a study from Harvard Business School that found something striking. The damage done by one toxic employee, like someone who manipulates, cuts corners, or destabilizes trust, is often greater than the benefit added by a strong performer.

It doesn't just stop with them. That kind of behavior spreads. Organiza-tional psychology research shows that unethical norms can be contagious. When people see that bad behavior is tolerated, or even rewarded, they start to adjust. They shift their standards to survive. What once felt unthinkable starts to look normal.

Bit by bit, the culture shifts. Accountability weakens. The sense of what's okay starts to blur.

That's when your compass matters most. Not when things are calm, but when the environment around you starts to pull in the wrong direction. That internal orientation becomes your anchor. And sometimes, it's the only thing keeping you from drifting with the current.

A LIFE LIVED:

When the Compass Falters

This story is hard to tell. Mostly because it doesn't have a clean ending. There's no redemption arc or tidy lesson at the end. To be honest, it goes against what I shared earlier. In Chapter 7, I talked about learning through difficulty and how some of the hardest moments become foundations. But this is different.

THE COMPASS LOOP

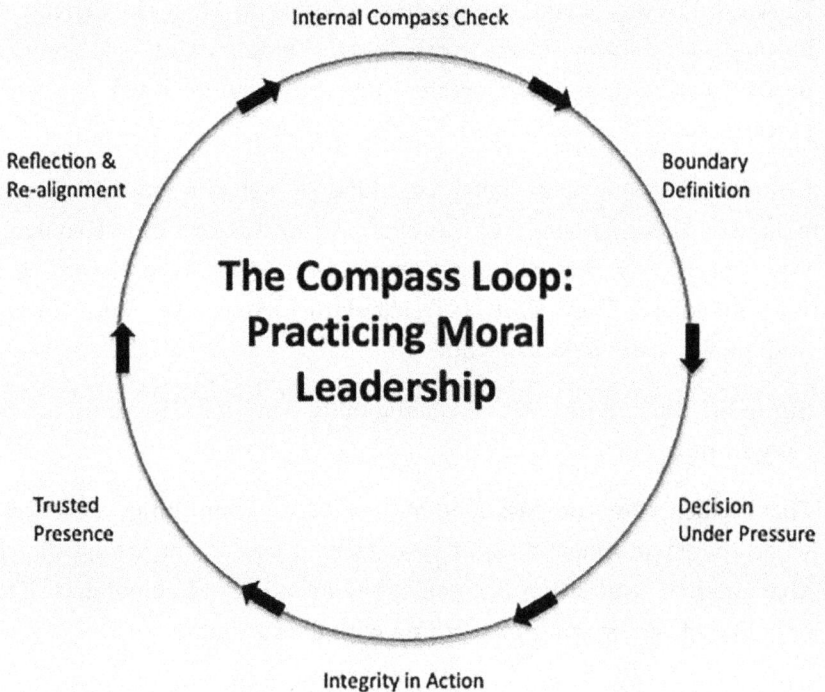

Internal Compass Check

Reflection & Re-alignment

Boundary Definition

The Compass Loop: Practicing Moral Leadership

Trusted Presence

Decision Under Pressure

Integrity in Action

Figure 8: The Compass Loop shows moral leadership as an ongoing cycle rather than a single moment of choice. Beginning with an inner-compass check and boundary setting, it moves through decisions under pressure to visible integrity, trusted presence, and reflective realignment—then starts again, reminding leaders to keep values in play at every turn.

THE COMPASS LOOP:
PRACTICING MORAL LEADERSHIP

This circle illustrates moral leadership as an ongoing practice rather than a one-time decision. It begins at the top with an Internal Compass Check, a quiet moment to ask, What do I truly stand for here? From that clarity you draw Boundary Definition, naming the non-negotiables before circumstances test them. Next comes Decision Under Pressure, when competing goals, time limits, or outside voices press in. If the earlier steps were honest, you can move through the squeeze without drifting.

After the choice is made, Integrity in Action turns conviction into visible behavior; people see that the values you claim are the values you live. Over time, this consistency creates Trusted Presence, a reputation for steadiness that gives others courage to act ethically as well. Finally, you enter Reflection & Re-alignment, noticing where your actions matched the compass and where they slipped. Any missteps feed back into the next Internal Compass Check, closing the loop and beginning the cycle anew.

Leadership strength, then, isn't rigid certainty; it's the discipline to keep traveling this loop, especially when the stakes are high.

REFLECTION PROMPT

Where in your current work are you skipping a step of the loop—and what small practice would help you bring it back into view?

This is about the kind of failure that doesn't build anything. The kind that just leaves a mark.

There were two moments. One was personal. One was professional. They came at very different times in my life. But in both, the pattern was the same. I ignored the compass. I crossed a line I had drawn. I didn't hold the boundary.

People got hurt. People I cared about. There's no undoing that part.

I was forgiven. Time passed. I kept moving. But those moments didn't fade. They're still with me. Sometimes they show up as reflection. Other times, they come back as shame. There's a quiet weight to carrying regret, and it's heavy.

A friend said something once that I've never forgotten. He said, "A mirror is like trust. Once it's broken, you can piece it back together. But the cracks don't go away."

Those cracks have taught me a few things. Things I carry into leadership now.

First, I need to root my compass in something that holds steady. Something bigger than me. For me, that's my faith. Since I've done that, I haven't felt lost in the same way and my compass hasn't faltered again.

Second, there isn't a separation between the personal and the professional. We don't switch compasses when we switch settings. We carry the same one into every room. Who we are shows up everywhere.

Third, the test never announces itself. The moment comes fast. It doesn't give you time to prepare. You won't rise to meet your ideals in that moment. You'll drop to the level of what you already know. The clarity you've already built. That's why boundaries have to be defined ahead of time, and they have to be firm enough to stand when the moment asks for them.

This story isn't about getting back up. It's about waking up. Realizing that a moral compass isn't just a guide for decisions. It's also a way of protecting something inside you. Something that can't be rebuilt if it's lost.

We don't get to choose every situation. We don't always get to shape the landscape. But we do get to choose how we walk through it.

More often than not, that's what defines leadership. Not the plans or the budgets or the titles. But the quiet choices. The ones made in the moments no one else sees. The ones that say, *This matters, even if I'm the only one acting like it does.*

Your compass won't look exactly like mine. Your boundaries will reflect your convictions. That's okay. What matters is that you've taken the time to name them. You carry them with you when things get uncertain. You know how to hold them steady when it counts.

In the end, the leaders who make the biggest difference aren't the ones who know the most or win the fastest. They're the ones who stay grounded in something real. The ones who lead from principle. Not perfectly. But consistently. And that makes all the difference.

PUTTING IT TO WORK: THREE DIMENSIONS OF APPLICATION

Industry

If you're leading inside an organization, one of the most important things you can do is make the moral expectations clear. Say them out loud. Make them visible in both policy and practice.

When people know where the ethical lines are and see those lines being respected, they start to trust the structure around them.

That trust lowers the risk of drift. It lowers the risk of public fallout too. When expectations are shared and leaders are consistent in how they model them, the organization becomes more stable. More aligned. More able to handle pressure without spinning out.

Ethics, when practiced this way, become part of the cultural fabric. Not a separate layer. Not a compliance box. But something woven into how people work together.

Professional Career

At the personal level, it helps to get very clear on what matters to you in practice rather than just theory. What are your non-negotiables? What lines are you not willing to cross, no matter what the opportunity might be?

Take the time to write them down if you need to, because that act of naming them helps lock them in.

Here's the thing: when pressure comes, you won't have time to build clarity. You'll have to act with the clarity you already have, and the gap between impulse and integrity is often determined by how much work you've done in advance.

Personal Life

Then there's the bigger view. The one that holds both work and everything outside of it.

It's tempting to think of your professional self as separate from who you are in private. But over time, that split becomes hard to manage. It asks too much of your energy. And people notice. Especially the people closest to you.

The more consistent your compass is across the parts of your life, the more trust you build with others *and* with yourself. That kind of consistency becomes a quiet kind of strength. One that helps you stay rooted when everything else feels like it's shifting.

9

THE DANGER OF AI

I've spent most of my career moving between two different spaces. One is shaped by the rhythm and pressure of everyday business. The other is slower and more analytical; it's the academic world where I try to make sense of how innovation actually happens.

I've learned a lot from going back and forth between them. You start to see certain patterns. You start to notice when things don't quite add up. Especially when the excitement around something starts to drown out the slower, harder work of understanding it. That's where I think we are now with artificial intelligence.

I want to say up front that I'm not someone who's afraid of AI. I use it. I teach with it. I write with it. I've seen how powerful and helpful it can be.

But the part that worries me doesn't usually make it into the headlines. It's something quieter, something that creeps in around the edges. It's the way AI is starting to change how we show up as leaders. Not in a deliberate, dramatic way. It's smaller than that. Slower. Which is maybe why it's more dangerous.

The real concern, at least for me, isn't that AI will take our place. It's that it might start to change us without us really noticing. That we'll slowly, quietly, begin to let go of the parts of leadership that are hardest to describe but most essential to keep. The things AI can't do are exactly the things we most need from each other.

Here's the concern in clearer terms: The real risk isn't that AI will replace leaders. It's that we'll start leading like machines; defaulting to patterns, avoiding ambiguity, and outsourcing the very judgment we're meant to bring.

WHAT AI CAN'T DO (AND WHY IT MATTERS)

AI is remarkably good at picking up patterns and doing something useful with them. It can pull things together, sort them, reorganize them, and make something that looks new from things that already exist. It can do all of that fast, but speed isn't the same as depth, and synthesis isn't the same as seeing.

AI is designed for environments where cause-and-effect logic works well. Where patterns are stable, and outcomes are relatively predictable.

But leadership often doesn't live in those conditions. Leadership lives in uncertainty, where you don't yet know what matters most, and where predictions don't hold.

There are things AI just can't do. Not now, and maybe not ever.

It can't pick up on something faint and still-forming, like what people sometimes call a weak signal, because it hasn't already happened a hundred times before. It can't feel anything, so it can't draw meaning from emotions or use them as a guide for what matters. It doesn't know how to weigh competing values, or how to act when the right choice is unclear and none of the options feel clean. AI can't build trust. It can't care. It can't make someone feel understood. And it can't walk people through uncertainty with any real sense of vision or steadiness.

These aren't nice-to-have qualities. They're not what gets added on after the "real" work of leadership is done. They are the work. Especially when things are messy or unclear or on the edge of changing.

Here's the thing that feels hard to say out loud, but may be important: as AI becomes more helpful in all the straightforward ways by helping us communicate, process, and decide, it becomes easier to lean on it in the ways that feel less risky. Easier to defer. To follow. To let the harder parts of leadership slide just a little.

At first, that shift might feel like efficiency. Like you're freeing up space for what matters. But over time, it has a cost. We start to lose the habits that keep us close to our judgment. We stop listening as carefully. We stop noticing things that don't show up on a dashboard. We become a little more comfortable with surface-level thinking. Once those muscles start to weaken, it's hard to get them back.

I don't think this is theoretical. It's already happening in small ways. I see people choosing AI summaries instead of sitting down to write their own reflections. I see teams relying on dashboards and scorecards instead of picking up the phone or walking down the hall. Leaders start trusting models more than their own sense of things. These aren't huge decisions. They're the kind that are easy to justify. But they add up. And slowly, the role of a leader starts to shift. Less about interpreting and more about executing. Less about listening and more about managing inputs and outputs.

AI is comforting in a way. Especially if you like to think in terms of cause and effect. If you like things to be clean. It gives the feeling that every problem has a logic to it. That if you just feed it enough data, it will give you a direction. But leadership doesn't really work like that. It's rarely clean. It's full of contradiction, and emotion, and uncertainty. It takes a kind of reasoning that moves across different modes, strategic, yes, but also relational, and sometimes ethical in ways that are hard to define.

When we give too much ground to AI, we don't just move faster. We narrow the frame. And the risk isn't just that we make a mistake. It's that we stop seeing people. Or context. Or the deeper reasons behind what we're doing.

The Judgment Paradox

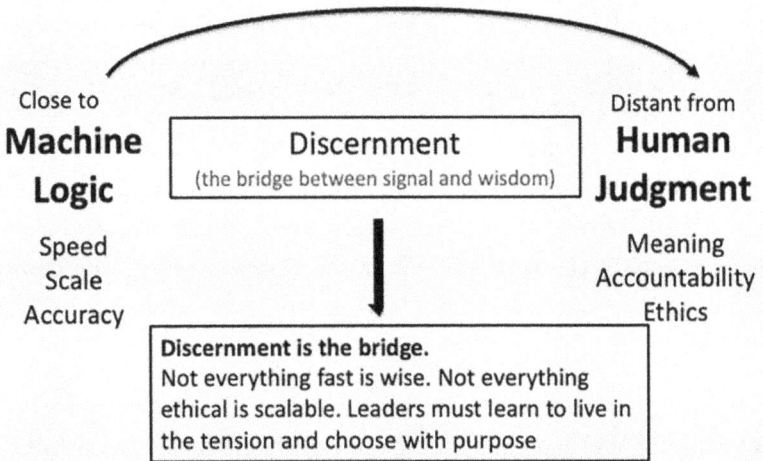

Close to

**Machine
Logic**

Speed
Scale
Accuracy

Discernment
(the bridge between signal and wisdom)

Distant from

**Human
Judgment**

Meaning
Accountability
Ethics

Discernment is the bridge.
Not everything fast is wise. Not everything
ethical is scalable. Leaders must learn to live in
the tension and choose with purpose

Figure 9: The Moral Drift Map

Figure 9: Algorithms deliver speed, scale, and statistical certainty, but they
stop short of meaning. Discernment is the human bridge and leaders must
translate machine signal through context, consequence, and character to
turn raw output into wise, accountable action.

THE JUDGMENT PARADOX

At first glance, the diagram looks like a simple tug-of-war; Machine Logic anchoring one side, Human Judgment the other. In practice, though, it's more like a circulatory loop. Algorithms excel at speed, scale, and statistical certainty; they spot recurring patterns faster than any human can. Yet none of those advantages tells us what the pattern means or whether acting on it will serve customers, employees, or society tomorrow. That interpretive gap is where leadership either rises or quietly abdicates.

The central band, Discernment, names the work that can't be automated. It asks three linked questions: Context (What hidden factors shaped this data?), Consequence (Who is helped or harmed if we follow it?), and Character (Does this choice align with the story we're trying to live?). Leaders travel the curved arrow over and over: drawing on machine insight, translating it through lived values, then feeding the learning back into smarter, more responsible systems. Skipping the loop creates two risks: Efficiency Drift, decisions so optimized they ignore nuance, and Ethical Paralysis, hand-wringing that never scales. The goal is neither surrender nor suspicion, but an active partnership in which data sharpens wisdom and wisdom humanizes data.

REFLECTION PROMPT

Think of an AI-informed recommendation you've received recently. What context, consequence, and character questions could you ask before accepting or rejecting it? How might those answers refine the final decision?

THE MUSCLE MEMORY OF LEADERSHIP

Leading well isn't something you're born knowing how to do. It takes work. And not the flashy kind. The kind that happens quietly, consistently, over time. Listening when it would be easier to speak. Sitting with a problem long enough to feel its shape rather than forcing it into an answer. Staying open to discomfort long enough to understand what it might be pointing to. Learning to notice what others miss, it's not that you're smarter, it's because you've been practicing the noticing. These small, repeated acts become more than skills. They form a kind of instinct. A leadership muscle memory you can trust when things get uncertain.

That kind of depth doesn't come from speed. It doesn't come from knowing the answer. It comes from presence and repetition. Research in decision science and organizational behavior suggests that durable judgment is built through *active engagement*; cycles of experience, reflection, feedback, and refinement.

According to Kahneman and Klein, two scholars often on opposite sides of the intuition debate, real expertise in uncertain domains requires both accumulated exposure and the right kind of feedback loops. In short, you don't just need time. You need *attentive time*. You need friction. You need context. You need to be close enough to the work that it shapes you.

But AI changes the rhythm of that practice. It doesn't force you to stop learning. It just makes it easier not to start. It offers the impression of wisdom without the effort. The illusion of competence without the risk of being wrong.

Because it moves so fast, and so cleanly, it can start to feel like a better version of leadership. One that's more efficient. More rational. Less exposed.

It often begins with something helpful. Using AI to take notes after a meeting. Then maybe to organize your thoughts before a difficult conversation. Soon it's helping you draft emails, prep for presentations, analyze feedback, or structure decisions.

None of these uses is inherently wrong. But if we aren't paying attention, they shift something underneath. They let us skip the slow parts. The wandering parts. The human parts.

And those are the parts that leadership is made of.

When we let AI do too much of the interpretive work, we lose contact with the process that sharpens us. We begin to move more efficiently, but less meaningfully. We feel smarter, but we become thinner. The leadership muscle we built by paying attention starts to weaken from disuse.

It's not just about craft. It's about calibration. It's about losing the ability to tell when something's off. Just like a musician who stops playing might still know the notes but loses their feel for phrasing, a leader who stops thinking deeply might still perform the role, but they stop recognizing when something no longer fits.

That friction, that moment of unease, is a form of wisdom. Decision theorists call them "somatic markers." It's the nervous system saying, "You've been here before. This didn't go well." That cue doesn't live in a model. It lives in the body, and AI can't feel it.

We need that friction. Especially when the stakes are high and the future is uncertain. Because it's not just uncertainty that's the problem; it's complexity. It's situations where the rules don't hold and the map doesn't match the terrain.

In those environments, what matters most often isn't what you know, it's how close you're willing to stay to what's unfolding. That's where effectual leadership shows up, in the movement that happens when there's just enough to go on, and enough feedback to act. Enough trust to try.

That's why repetition matters. Not just doing the same thing over and over but *staying present* through cycles of action, reflection, and adaptation. According to work in complexity theory and adaptive leadership, what distinguishes great leaders isn't certainty. It's elasticity. It's the ability to shift reasoning modes and draw from strategy and intuition, from data and values, from experience and emerging sense. That capacity doesn't come from streamlining. It comes from *staying in the mess long enough to learn something real.*

So yes, AI can help. It can summarize. It can structure. It can support. But it can also flatten. What gets flattened first is usually the most human layer: the quiet knowing, the subtle reading of the room, the unspoken patterns behind someone's resistance. The slow building of trust that doesn't show up on any dashboard.

That's why this moment matters because AI will quietly reshape us through a steady erosion. We start giving up the hardest parts of leadership, and we tell ourselves it's productivity. We start leaning on the cleanest logic, and we forget that complexity doesn't work like that. We lose something bit by bit until what's left still looks like leadership, but no longer feels like it.

LEADERSHIP IN THE PRESENCE OF INTELLIGENCE

AI tends to make sense to us because it fits a kind of logic we've come to trust. It sees patterns. It looks at what's already happened and guesses what might happen next. That's causal reasoning: if this, then that. AI is very good at it. It's designed to be.

But most of the systems we lead in, organizations, teams, and communities, don't always follow that kind of logic. Not reliably. Not cleanly. They're messier. More relational. Less predictable. What works in one situation might fall apart in the next, even if the surface looks the same. And what matters most often isn't measurable at all.

That's why this broader model of leadership matters. Leadership has never been about just one way of knowing. It has always required multiple lenses. Different kinds of attention. Different forms of reasoning that can sit alongside each other without needing to collapse into one clean answer.

So when I talk about multi-dimensional leadership, I'm pointing to that space. The space where different intelligences are in conversation. Where strategy doesn't just mean hitting targets, but staying aligned with something that lasts. Where analysis doesn't stop at what the numbers say, it asks where the numbers came from. Where relationships aren't separate from logic, but part of it. Where values aren't just slogans, they're constraints on what we're willing to do.

Each of these dimensions brings something essential.

The **strategic** helps us think in arcs, not just snapshots.

What is this really serving? What future are we shaping?

The **analytical** helps us stay grounded.

What's missing here? What assumptions are hiding under the surface?

The **relational** helps us stay connected.

How does this land on the people it touches? What does trust look like here?

The **ethical** pulls us back when the other dimensions start to drift.

What are we saying yes to without meaning to? What are we trading away?

These aren't theoretical questions. They show up in real choices, like the one that happened at Amazon, when they built an AI tool to help with hiring. It learned from historical resumes exactly as it was designed to. It started filtering out candidates who'd gone to women's colleges because the training data reflected a history of bias and that bias got embedded, quietly, into the system's logic. No one prompted the AI to filter, it just did.

The problem wasn't just with the tool. It was with the silence around it. The way the system was trusted without being questioned. No one asked the deeper questions because the output looked clean. The model looked confident. So people went along.

That's what we have to watch for. That drift. That moment when we stop asking and start assuming.

That's where leadership comes in, to hold AI in a larger frame. To ask:

What is this tool actually showing us? And what is it leaving out?

Because prediction is not decision. And pattern is not purpose.

Leadership still lives in the space between those things, in the stretch between what the system tells you and what the moment actually calls for. It's in that stretch that your presence matters most. That your attention becomes a kind of offering.

AI can help. It can inform. But it cannot choose.

That choice is still yours. And the weight of that choice isn't a flaw in the system.

It's the reason you're needed.

CLOSING REFLECTION

AI isn't the threat. Forgetting how to lead is.

The real danger of AI is not that it will outthink us, it's that we'll stop thinking well in its presence. We'll surrender the work of interpretation. We'll quiet the internal questions. We'll trade context for convenience. In doing so, we risk becoming operators of a system rather than stewards of its impact.

This doesn't happen all at once. It happens slowly, through tiny deferrals. We stop asking where a recommendation came from. We follow the cleanest output. We assume the system has already done the hard work. And before we know it, we're managing confidence, not complexity.

Leadership in the age of intelligence won't be defined by who has the most automation, the most data, or the most impressive dashboards. It won't be defined by prediction or even speed. It will be defined by something far older and far rarer: the ability to stay grounded in human judgment, especially when the machine seems to know more. It will be defined by our ability to stay in relationship with complexity, with each other, and with the responsibility to choose.

The most effective leaders going forward will be the ones who remember what can't be automated at all.

A LIFE LIVED:

The Siren's Call: Staying Human in the Age of AI

When I first started working with AI, I was caught off guard by how useful it was. I used it for drafts, for summaries, and even for bits of code. It felt like I had this endlessly available partner who could pick up whatever thread I gave it and run with it. There was something exciting about that. And also something disorienting.

At first, I leaned on it more than I expected to. It made things easier. Faster. But over time, something started to shift in a way I didn't like. When I let AI do the first pass, I found it harder to hear the thinking behind my voice. It wasn't that the words were wrong. It was more subtle than that. They just didn't feel like mine.

Eventually, I had to pause so that I could recenter and find my way back into the work. That's when it became clear to me that AI isn't neutral. It doesn't just support your process, it shapes it. It tunes itself to your voice, but only if you're still there. If you're not, it can start to flatten you out. Make you sound more polished than present.

What changed things for me was a simple shift. I stopped asking, "What does the system think?" and started asking something different: "What role does this system have in the choice I'm making?" That question helped me find my footing again. It moved me out of passivity and into discernment.

I want to be honest here: I'm not a technical expert. I don't have a background in computer science. I can't explain exactly how training data works or how neural networks process language. What I do know and what I've spent my whole career trying to understand is how people work. How we make meaning. How we move through complexity. And how we lead when the answers aren't obvious.

When I first started using AI, I fell into the same trap many people do. I assumed that if the tool was smart enough, it could make the decisions for me. That it would know better. I could outsource the hard parts of leadership to a system that didn't get tired or uncertain. There was a kind of hope in that. And also a kind of avoidance.

But it didn't work.

What I got back were ideas that sounded right but felt off. Suggestions that looked polished but missed the point. The deeper parts, the human parts, weren't there. The more I let AI take the lead, the less connected I felt. To the work. To the people. To myself.

Things started to shift when I stopped treating AI like a crystal ball and started seeing it as something more collaborative. More like a sparring partner. Or a mirror. Something that could help me think but couldn't think for me.

I started working with a different mindset. One that puts presence at the center. That made room for intuition and interpretation. I didn't stop using AI. I just stopped asking it to carry what it couldn't.

That's where this idea of multi-dimensional leadership came into focus for me. The kind of leadership that doesn't rely on one way of knowing. It can move between logic and feeling. Between what's been done and what might be possible.

AI can support that kind of leadership, but only if we're clear on what we're asking of it.

Now, I use AI differently depending on the context I'm in. When I'm thinking strategically, I might use it to surface patterns I hadn't seen or to play out possible scenarios.

When I'm coaching or facilitating, I might use it to reflect back themes or tensions, but I'm always listening for what it misses.

When I'm in a more creative place, it helps me move quickly to throw out rough ideas and see what sticks. It's not driving the process. It's part of it.

But no matter the use, the turning point was always the same. I stopped looking for answers. I started looking for alignment. I stopped depending on the system. I started being intentional about how to include it.

AI can be fast. It can be smart. But it can't tell you what matters. It can't choose your direction. Only you can do that.

That's why I don't think the future of leadership belongs to the most technical or the most data-literate. I think it belongs to the people who can stay grounded in their humanness while working alongside intelligence. The ones who are willing to interpret instead of deferring. Who know how to be in relationship with the tool, but not in service to it.

The work is still ours, and the meaning is, too.

PUTTING IT TO WORK: THREE DIMENSIONS OF APPLICATION

Industry

One of the first things I recommend is to step back and really look at where AI is already shaping decisions within your industry. This goes beyond the obvious areas like automation or data analysis.

Pay particular attention to the decisions it's involved in, especially the ones that touch people directly. I'm talking about areas like hiring, promotion, pricing, and personalization. We see AI being used to help businesses decide who gets a job, who gets a raise, or even how much a customer should pay. These are deeply personal decisions. And yet, AI is being asked to make them.

When you see these kinds of applications, I think it's worth asking: What kind of leadership logic is at work here? Is this decision being made analytically, with a focus on efficiency and data? Is it relational, meaning it takes into account how people are affected and how those relationships shift over time? Is it ethical, questioning whether the right values are being upheld? Or is it simply computational, focusing on patterns, numbers, and outputs without much regard for the deeper context?

Once you start asking these questions, you'll find that the answer often lies somewhere in between. But here's the key: As leaders, we need to build systems and review processes that put the final accountability back into human hands.

If AI is going to be involved in decisions, we cannot allow those decisions to be fully automated. We must have review protocols in place that ensure there's always a person who can interpret, question, and ultimately take responsibility for the decision. Make "interpretive fluency" a leadership competency. It's not just about knowing how to read data anymore. It's about knowing how to make sense of it, in all its complexity, and to challenge it when necessary.

Professional Career

The world is moving fast, and you'll likely find yourself using AI tools sooner or later. But the question is: how are you using them? Are you simply taking their outputs at face value, or are you taking the time to understand what's behind them?

The real challenge lies in practicing interpretive fluency. That's a term I use to describe the ability to critically engage with the outputs AI gives you, more than just an understanding of how it works, but also learning to question what it produces.

Ask yourself: *What's missing from the data I'm seeing? Who might be excluded or overlooked because the system doesn't have access to their experiences? Does the recommendation align with my values, and if not, why not?*

It's not enough to just use AI as a tool. It's important to show others how you're using it too. If you want to lead effectively in a world increasingly shaped by machines, you need to demonstrate how AI is part of your decision-making process, not the whole of it.

AI is just one voice in the room, and that's a voice you must be able to integrate with your own. You, as a leader, are the one who decides what path to take, not the machine.

By practicing and demonstrating interpretive fluency in your work, you're not only becoming a more thoughtful leader, you're helping to shape a culture of decision-making that doesn't rely solely on AI for answers, but uses it as a tool to deepen understanding.

Personal Life

It's easy to think of AI as a problem that only exists in the professional or industrial space. But the truth is, it's becoming more and more a part of our everyday lives.

That's something we need to think about: how technology is starting to shape the way we live, even when we're not in the office or at work. So, think about this: how can you teach your family, your friends, and even your community to notice when technology feels too confident?

This isn't about demonizing AI, but about encouraging a kind of mindfulness. Help those around you recognize when technology starts to dictate what feels right or true and encourage them to pause and question. It's important to foster an attitude of curiosity instead of certainty. Ask questions. What is this technology really telling me? Is it serving my interests, or just feeding me information that makes me feel comfortable or validated?

When it comes to your kids, for example, it's vital to teach them that not everything can be predicted. Some of life's most important moments like love, learning, and meaning, cannot be reduced to data. These are the spaces where presence, connection, and wonder matter most. They don't need algorithms or predictions to guide them. By fostering curiosity, we protect the human aspects of life that no machine can replace.

In short, protect the parts of your life that should remain uncertain, that should remain human. These are not data problems. They are experiences, and they thrive in environments where questions are more important than answers, and presence matters more than prediction.

10

WHY LOGIC MATTERS

M ost leaders I've worked with didn't set out to use the wrong logic. That's not how it happens. Usually, it comes from habit. Or from pressure. Or just from the way things have always worked before.

You're in a situation that feels familiar, so you go with the tools you know. You plan. You predict. You try to chart a path. And often, that's enough.

But not always.

I remember sitting with a founder once, someone deeply capable, someone who had built their company from scratch. They were preparing to expand, and everything about their posture said planning. They wanted projections, timelines, metrics. All of which made sense until the environment shifted.

Suddenly, their customers started behaving differently. A new competitor entered. Supply chains moved in strange ways. And the plan stopped working. But instead of adjusting, they doubled down. They made a better plan. A tighter forecast. Still, things got worse because they were using the wrong kind of logic for the moment they were in. These were smart people but they only understood an approach centered on data-driven prediction.

That conversation stuck with me because it wasn't unusual. It was something I had heard before.

I've seen it happen over and over, in boardrooms, startups, and classrooms. Leaders rely on prediction when the ground is already moving. Or, in other cases, embrace improvisation when what's needed is structure and sequence.

In both scenarios, the outcome is usually frustration, but the cause isn't bad leadership. It's misaligned reasoning. Once you learn to see it, you start to notice just how common it is.

Most leaders default to a single mode. Often it's the predictive, causal one because that's what many organizations reward. Set a target, make a plan, execute with discipline.

When conditions are stable, that works well. But when the situation changes, when uncertainty rises or the future becomes hard to predict, the same habits that once created progress can quietly start to create drag.

That's where this chapter begins.

If there's one throughline to multi-dimensional leadership, it's this: the ability to shift how you think, not just what you do. To recognize that different moments call for different forms of logic. To develop the awareness and stamina to move between them without losing your footing.

So this chapter isn't about choosing one approach over another. It's not about arguing that effectual thinking is better or that causal logic is outdated. It's about learning to notice which kind of reasoning fits which kind of moment and being willing to switch, even when it's uncomfortable.

In practice, the ability to choose the right kind of logic is what allows leaders to stay grounded. It's what keeps teams from stalling. Over time, it becomes one of the most important disciplines a leader can build, not because it solves every problem, but because it helps you see what kind of problem you're actually in.

THE TWO LOGICS OF LEADERSHIP

There are two core ways that leaders tend to make decisions. Most of the time, they're not named out loud. They're just patterns we slip into: ways of thinking that feel natural, because they've worked before. But when we name them, we start to get more choice. More flexibility. More clarity about when to use which.

Much of what I've described earlier about effectual thinking, moral grounding, and adaptive presence, comes into sharper focus here, where we look more directly at the logics that sit underneath those behaviors.

Causal Reasoning

Causal reasoning starts with a goal. It's the kind of logic that says, "Here's where we're trying to go. Now let's figure out how to get there." It works from prediction. From past data. From what's already been proven to work. You define the outcome, then reverse-engineer the steps to get there.

This is the logic that drives most planning processes. It's behind strategy decks, product roadmaps, and five-year growth targets. It's incredibly effective in environments that are stable and well understood. And when market behavior is predictable, inputs and outputs are consistent, and you're scaling something that's already been built.

When I was helping one company expand a known service line into new geographic regions, we leaned heavily on causal reasoning. We knew the customer. We had solid data. The logistics were tight. What we needed was structure, sequencing, and precision. That's where causal logic thrives.

There's nothing wrong with it. In fact, it's essential. But it has limits, especially when the environment is changing faster than your models can keep up.

Years later, I learned that this way of moving through uncertainty had a name: effectual thinking. Originally developed through research with expert entrepreneurs, the framework gave language to what I, and many others, had already been doing.

Effectual Reasoning

Effectual reasoning starts somewhere else. Instead of starting with a goal, it starts with what you already have: your means. Your experience. Your network. Your team. Your credibility. And it asks a different question: "Given what I've got, what could I build?"

This logic doesn't rely on prediction. It relies on control of your next step *today*, instead of trying to predict an uncertain tomorrow. It's about working with uncertainty, not trying to eliminate it. Instead of assuming the future is knowable, it assumes the future is shapeable.

I spent a good portion of my life working this way without realizing it had a name. As a young entrepreneur, I didn't have perfect information or well-formed strategies. I had motion. I had relationships. I had instincts.

Most of the time, I was figuring it out as I went. For years, I thought that was a flaw. That I was somehow missing the discipline other leaders had.

For a long time, I didn't have a name for how I was working. I just knew I wasn't building from prediction. I was moving from what I had: my relationships, my instincts, my resources, and adjusting along the way. It wasn't clean or linear, but it kept me in motion. Eventually, I came to see that what I was doing wasn't a lack of discipline. It was a different kind of logic, one that co-creates the future rather than forecasts it.

Effectual logic thrives in ambiguity. In places where you don't yet know the path. In early-stage ventures, or when a team is working under constraint, or when the future is just too unpredictable to plan around. It asks leaders to move anyway. To stay in motion even when clarity hasn't arrived.

TWO DIFFERENT LOGICS OF LEADERSHIP	
Causal Reasoning	**Effectual Reasoning**
Starts with a goal. "Here's where we're going."	Starts with what you have. "Given who I am, what I know, and who I know, what can I do?"
Works from prediction. Assumes the future can be forecasted and planned for.	Works from control. Assumes the future is shaped by what you do with what's in your hands.
Often used in stable, structured environments.	Often used in ambiguous, fast-changing, or early-stage environments
Follows a linear path: set the goal, build the plan, execute the plan.	Follows a looping path: act, learn, adjust, repeat.
Focuses on efficiency and optimization.	Focuses on adaptability and co-creation.
Assumes clear outcomes and measurable success.	Assumes outcomes will emerge and may shift along the way.
Tends to rely on past data and proven methods.	Tends to rely on relationships, instincts, and available means.
Well-suited for scaling, replicating, and executing known models.	Well-suited for exploring, iterating, and creating something new.
Helps when clarity is high, and resources are aligned.	Helps when clarity is low, and resources are limited or evolving.

WHEN THE WRONG LOGIC LEADS US ASTRAY

One of the things I've seen, over and over, in classrooms, boardrooms, and in my history, is that the problem usually isn't that leaders don't have a plan. It's that they're using the wrong kind of plan for the environment they're in. Or, just as often, they're avoiding structure altogether when the moment calls for it.

Most of the time, it's not because they're unaware. It's because the environment shifted, and no one noticed. Or maybe they noticed, but they weren't sure what to do with that noticing.

We all have a default way of leading. Some of us like clarity, direction, and a timeline. We find comfort in structure. Others lean more toward iteration. We want to try, test, learn. Neither one of those instincts is a flaw.

But either one can become a liability when we apply it to the wrong context. When that happens, the work doesn't just slow down, it starts to feel misaligned. People begin to sense that something's off, even if they can't explain what it is.

I remember a time when I watched a leadership team continue to operate as if their five-year strategy was still holding, even though every signal in the system had changed. The market was shifting. Customer expectations were evolving. Their workforce was asking for different things.

But the strategy stayed fixed. Not because they didn't care. Not because they weren't paying attention. But because they equated discipline with consistency.

For a while, it worked. Until it didn't. The longer they tried to predict their way through uncertainty, the more stuck they became. The indicators were there: declining responsiveness, slower decision cycles, quieter meetings, but they stayed the course because switching logic felt like abandoning the plan.

This kind of misalignment is surprisingly common. In a 2021 McKinsey survey of over 1,200 global executives, seventy percent reported that their strategic planning cycles were still based on linear, predictive models, even though only twenty-three percent felt that those models reflected the actual volatility of their markets. The disconnect isn't new, but the pace of change has made it more visible.

On the other side, I've seen teams avoid structure altogether because they've been told to "stay agile" or "keep iterating." There's value in that, but when adaptation becomes unanchored, it can start to feel like drift. The vision gets blurry. People start to lose sight of what they're building toward.

Eventually, the team wears down because the absence of structure becomes its own kind of weight. They are capable and they care, but they are only comfortable navigating in a structured environment. A 2022 study in the *Journal of Organizational Behavior* found that teams working in environments with high ambiguity but low structure experienced significantly lower levels of psychological safety and sustained focus. The issue wasn't ambiguity itself, it was that no one named the logic in the room.

These aren't stories about incompetence or failure. These stories are about mismatch. About what happens when the reasoning behind our decisions doesn't fit the conditions we're working in. And they're more common than we tend to admit.

You can usually feel it before you can name it. The plan keeps stalling. The meetings start to loop. People are working, but it's not clear what success looks like anymore. Or maybe you're avoiding a decision because none of the options come with guarantees.

These are signals. They don't always mean you've chosen the wrong approach. But they often mean it's time to check. To step back. To ask whether the logic that got you here is still the logic that will carry you forward.

That's the moment where leadership becomes more layered because you need to adjust how you're reasoning. You don't need to overhaul everything and you don't need to start from scratch. Just from a different kind of footing.

There's a term in cognitive science called "cognitive entrenchment." It refers to what happens when experienced professionals become overly reliant on familiar mental models, even in the face of new or contradictory data. It's not stubbornness. It's habit. It's exactly why logic-switching isn't about intelligence, it's about awareness. The willingness to notice when the environment is asking for something different and the courage to shift.

It's not about blaming yourself for misreading the moment. It's about learning how to recognize that the rules have changed. What worked before might not work now. That's okay because the real work of leadership isn't about always being right. It's about being responsive. And responsible. At the same time.

THE SKILL OF LOGIC-SWITCHING

Most people I've worked with aren't strangers to the idea of planning. They know how to make a roadmap, set a target, and break it into parts. Most of them aren't strangers to adaptability either. They've learned to respond when the unexpected shows up.

But what's less common, at least in my experience, is the habit of naming which kind of thinking they're using, and why.

That's really what "logic-switching" is about. It's not some elite capacity. It's not a personality trait. It's a discipline. A practice. Something that gets built over time, through paying attention. Not just to the problem in front of you, but to how you're approaching it. What assumptions you're carrying into the moment. What kind of reasoning you're defaulting to. And whether it still fits.

In my leadership work, I didn't name this right away. I moved between logics intuitively, sometimes planning, sometimes reacting, sometimes building from scratch with whatever I had.

But I didn't always see the switch as part of the work. I saw it as adaptation. Or grit. Or just doing what needed to be done. It wasn't until later, especially when I started teaching, that I began to understand it more clearly.

Once I saw it, I started to wonder why it wasn't being taught more deliberately. Why we didn't help leaders recognize that they were already switching, just not always with intention.

The skill begins with reflection. With slowing down enough to ask:

- "What kind of decision is this?"
- "Is this a moment that calls for prediction or for control over what I can shape right now?"
- "Am I working toward a known goal, or trying to discover what's possible with the means I have?"
- "Have I been here before, or is this uncharted territory?"

These questions don't give you a formula. But they give you a foothold. A place to stand long enough to make a more conscious move.

Mature leaders, the ones who've seen a few systems up close, don't usually abandon one logic in favor of the other. They don't become "causal thinkers" or "effectual operators." They learn how to carry both and to know which one to lead with, and when to shift.

The shift itself isn't just strategic, it's emotional. Changing how you lead often means letting go of something like clarity, confidence, control. It might mean admitting that the plan isn't working or that the plan isn't enough. It might mean holding the discomfort of moving forward without knowing exactly where you're going. It almost always means standing in front of your team and saying, out loud, "We're changing how we're thinking about this."

That moment can feel vulnerable. But in my experience, it's one of the most honest forms of leadership. You're not just showing that you have a plan, you're showing that you know how to think. That you're willing to respond to what's real. That kind of transparency often builds more trust than a polished strategy ever could.

CONTRASTING PATHS:
CAUSAL VS. EFFECTUAL REASONING

Causal Reasoning	Effectual Reasoning
Starts with a goal. "Here's where we're going."	Starts with what you have. "Given who I am, what I know, and who I know—what can I do?"
Works from prediction. Assumes the future can be forecasted and planned for.	Works from control. Assumes the future is shaped by what you do with what's in your hands.
Often used in stable, structured environments.	Often used in ambiguous, fast-changing, or early-stage environments.
Follows a linear path: set the goal, build the plan, execute the plan.	Follows a looping path: act, learn, adjust, repeat.
Focuses on efficiency and optimization.	Focuses on adaptability and co-creation.
Assumes clear outcomes and measurable success.	Assumes outcomes will emerge and may shift along the way.
Tends to rely on past data and proven methods.	Tends to rely on relationships, instincts, and available means.
Well-suited for scaling, replicating, and executing known models.	Well-suited for exploring, iterating, and creating something new.
Helps when clarity is high and resources are aligned.	Helps when clarity is low and resources are limited or evolving.

Figure 10: Causal reasoning charts a straight path from a predefined goal, relying on past data and linear plans to optimize efficiency when conditions are stable. Effectual reasoning begins with the means at hand, iterating through action-learn-adjust loops that create adaptable progress in uncertain or fast-changing environments.

TWO DIFFERENT LOGICS OF LEADERSHIP

The diagram pairs two columns to highlight the essential contrast between causal and effectual reasoning. Read it from left to right, row by row.

On the left, causal logic begins with a fixed destination. You pick a goal, gather past data, predict the path, and drive execution. The movement is linear—plan → sequence → optimize—so it thrives where markets are stable, resources are known, and success can be measured against clear targets. Think of launching a proven product into an additional region: assumptions are tested, variables are limited, and efficiency is king.

On the right, effectual logic flips the script. It starts with available means— your skills, network, assets—and asks, "What can we create from here?" The process is looping: act → learn → adjust. It leans on relationship-building and real-time feedback because the future is considered shapeable, not predictable. This approach shines in new ventures, crises, and fast-moving domains where waiting for perfect information would leave you standing still.

The rows in the center spell out the trade-offs. Causal logic offers clarity, efficiency, and scale but can lock a team into outdated maps when conditions shift. Effectual logic offers adaptability and discovery but, without eventual structure, can exhaust people who need milestones.

Seen together, the columns are less a choice than a compass: they remind leaders to match reasoning to context and to signal the switch when reality demands it. Mastery lies in moving fluidly between both sides rather than living exclusively in one.

REFLECTION PROMPT

Recall a recent decision. Did you lead with a fixed goal or with the means at hand? If conditions changed tomorrow, how might you pivot to the other logic without losing momentum—or trust?

So logic-switching isn't about abandoning discipline. It's about expanding what discipline includes. It means making room for multiple ways of reasoning to sit side by side. To let one take the lead when the conditions call for it, and to let the other step forward when things shift again. It means being able to hold both structure and motion. Both planning and emergence. Not as opposites, but as partners in the work.

That's the root of multi-dimensional leadership. Not mastery over every method, but the ability to switch with purpose. To notice what the moment is asking for and to move accordingly, with clarity and care.

LEADING OTHERS THROUGH THE SWITCH

One of the harder parts of logic-switching isn't doing it yourself. It's bringing others with you.

Most teams, in my experience, aren't trained to think this way. They've been taught to look for clarity. To expect consistency. To build around a plan and follow it. So when a leader changes direction in the kind of reasoning that's shaping the work, it can feel disorienting.

Sometimes it looks like whiplash. The team has been pushing toward a fixed target, and suddenly, the conversation turns. Now they're building from what they have. Now the goal is open-ended. Now they're exploring instead of executing. If that shift isn't named, it can sound like confusion. Or worse, like someone just changed the rules in the middle of the game.

That's why part of the discipline is learning how to frame the shift. It's to say out loud, "We've been in planning mode, and that made sense for a while. But the conditions have changed. The feedback we're getting doesn't match the assumptions we started with. So we're going to switch for a bit. We're going to move from prediction to exploration. From following the map to shaping the terrain as we go."

That kind of transparency takes practice. It can feel unnatural, especially in environments that prize certainty. But in my experience, teams don't need perfection. They need honesty. And they need to be invited into the logic, not just the outcome.

Research supports this. When leaders make their mental models visible, teams perform better because people are better able to interpret shifts and contribute meaningfully. It has little to do with leaders having all the answers.

Karl Weick's work on sensemaking is especially helpful here. He described leadership not as providing clarity in a traditional sense, but as offering cues that allow others to build shared understanding in the midst of uncertainty.

Weick's central idea, that people act and interpret at the same time, means that small moments of framing can have an outsized impact. A quiet signal. A well-timed explanation. Even just naming what's changing and why can help a team recalibrate.

Making the reasoning visible helps people reorient. It gives them a framework for why things feel different. It invites them to participate in the shift, rather than just react to it.

In the workshops I run with executive teams, this often becomes one of the most meaningful conversations. Leaders will say, "We've been operating with a causal mindset because it's what we know. But what if this part of the work actually needs something else?"

Once they name that possibility, the tone in the room shifts. People start to ask different questions. They stop trying to make the old model work and begin looking more closely at what's actually in front of them.

That's where collective momentum begins, with shared awareness instead of a top-down decision.

It's also where leadership deepens. Because now you're not just guiding action. You're guiding attention. Helping the group see the logic underneath the move, and giving them language to respond with more clarity and trust.

This kind of reasoning fluency, moving between logics and inviting others into that motion, isn't just a conceptual strength. It's a performance strength. A 2021 study published in *Organization Science* found that teams with greater "cognitive framing alignment" around ambiguity were more resilient and adaptive under stress because they knew how to respond together when prediction failed.

So the work here isn't just individual, it's relational. It's not just switching logics yourself. It's helping others move through the switch with you. Naming the change. Explaining the reasoning. Inviting reflection and creating enough space for people to adjust without losing their footing.

It doesn't have to be dramatic. Most of the time, it's just a pause. A short conversation. A quiet question like, "Does our current approach still match the moment we're in?"

That's often enough to open the door. And once it's open, people don't just follow. They start thinking differently too.

That's when a team becomes more than a group of operators. It becomes a learning system. One that can adapt because the group knows how to move together when the ground shifts.

PRACTICE EXAMPLES

By now, the concept of logic-switching might feel clear in theory. But the real test of this skill happens in practice, when the stakes are unclear, the path is murky, and the need for action presses in.

What follows are a few moments from my experience, places where the ability to shift reasoning made a difference. Not always cleanly. Not always in time. But often enough to notice.

When Causal Logic Saved the Day

Years ago, I was working with a founder who had recently shifted from early-stage growth to scaling. Up to that point, most of his decisions had been made in real time, based on gut instinct and relationships.

But as the team grew and investors came on board, that way of working started to strain. Deadlines were slipping. Priorities kept shifting. People were confused about who was deciding what. At one point, he said, "I'm still leading like we're ten people, but we're forty-five now."

We stepped back and built out a clearer causal structure: fixed goals, backward planning, defined roles, and timelines. He didn't love it. But he could see why it mattered.

Within six months, the team was delivering more consistently and with less friction. This wasn't about abandoning creativity. It was about recognizing that in this part of the business, the environment was stable enough to benefit from a predictive approach. Structure was the enabler. Causal reasoning gave them traction.

When Effectuation Unlocked Momentum

In a different case, I was advising a team at a large organization that had been tasked with building a new innovation function. They had been spinning for months, waiting on approvals, trying to write the perfect charter, getting stuck in planning mode. Eventually, in frustration, someone said, "We keep acting like this is a rollout, but no one knows what this is yet."

That was the signal. The context wasn't ready for prediction. What they needed was motion. We shifted to an effectual frame: Who's already interested? What could we prototype in the next few weeks? What relationships can we build that might shape this into something real?

That shift unlocked something. Within a month, they had a pilot running. Not perfect. Not polished. But real. Something people could see and respond to. That became the foundation for what came next. The causal logic came later, once they knew what they were building.

When the Switch Itself Was the Leadership Move

One of the most powerful moments I've seen happened in a boardroom. A leader I work with stood in front of her executive team and said, "We've been operating under the assumption that this problem is solvable through planning. But we've tried three versions of the plan, and none of them are working. I think we need to stop aiming for control and start asking what we can do with what we have."

She didn't have a new strategy yet. What she had was awareness and the courage to name it. That one sentence shifted the room. It didn't make things easier, but it made them more honest. From there, the team could start working in a new way. More adaptive. More relational. More real.

That was the moment leadership happened. Not in the decision itself, but in the switch. In naming the context. In helping others reframe what kind of reasoning the moment required.

NOVA-U: A PRACTICAL COMPASS FOR CHOOSING LOGIC

Over time, I found myself coming back to the same question in different rooms. Whether I was teaching, advising, or building alongside others, the question was this: "How do you know when to apply causal logic and when to shift toward effectual thinking?" Not in hindsight. Not as a thought exercise. But in real time, when the decision is still in front of you and the path isn't clear yet.

That's where NOVA-U came from. It wasn't born in a lab or built for publication. It came from the field. From watching leaders move through uncertainty. From seeing how often the real challenge isn't knowing the tools, it's knowing when to use them.

The idea behind NOVA-U is simple. It offers a way to assess the logic that fits the moment based on a single determining variable: "predictive validity." In plain terms, how much useful data do you have? And can that data reliably inform the next decision?

NOVA-U stands for **Navigating Opportunity, Volatility, Ambiguity, and Uncertainty**. It's not a formula. It's a guide. And it starts with a question:

"Can this environment be reliably predicted using the data we have?"

If the answer is yes, the patterns are strong, the precedent is clear, and the variables are relatively stable, then causal reasoning likely makes sense.Set the goal. Build the plan. Follow it.

But if the answer is no, if the data is incomplete, the environment is shifting, or the problem itself is still being defined, then you're probably better served by effectual logic. Start from your means. Build through interaction. Let the opportunity take shape through motion and learning.

In workshops, we walk through five core dimensions of assessment. They are not rigid rules. They are ways to read the environment:

- **Stability**: Is the context relatively consistent over time, or does it shift often?
- **Data sufficiency**: Do we have enough past information to build a reliable forecast?
- **Urgency**: Do we have time to plan thoroughly, or do we need to act now?
- **Stakeholder alignment**: Are roles and goals clear, or still in flux?
- **Constraint type**: Are we bounded by rules and structure, or shaped more by creative limits?

What NOVA-U does is hold up a mirror. It doesn't make the choice for you. It surfaces what's true in the moment so you can respond with intention.

One of the things I've learned over time is that logic-switching becomes a lot easier when you've got a shared vocabulary. Especially inside organizations.

Teams can learn to ask each other, "Where are we on the NOVA-U map right now?" or "Have we crossed into effectual territory?" That language softens resistance. It makes the shift less personal. Less about a change in direction and more about a change in conditions.

In practice, that's what makes a tool like NOVA-U useful. It doesn't give you certainty, but it will help you name the uncertainty with others and move forward anyway.

TYING IT BACK: HOW NOVA-U CONNECTS THE DOTS

If you've made it this far in the book, you've already seen these logics in action. You've read about Loyal Rebels who navigate internal tension by sensing when to challenge the system and when to stay grounded inside it.

You've seen how leaders move with a moral compass, especially when the clarity of data gives way to the fog of complexity.

You've walked through the behaviors of effectual leadership: those that begin with what is in your hands and evolve through motion, interaction, and learning.

What NOVA-U offers is a bridge. A way to connect those lived practices back to a decision point. Not in theory, but in the day-to-day moments where a leader has to ask: "What kind of reasoning belongs here?"

It helps make visible what might otherwise stay intuitive. It gives shape to something many experienced leaders already feel, but haven't always had the words to describe.

Earlier, we talked about how effectual logic often goes unnamed. People practice it without realizing it. They co-create. They improvise. They lean on relationships. Sometimes, they wonder if what they're doing counts as real leadership.

In Chapter 7, we explored how the effectual cycle brings that kind of leadership into focus and how it reflects a different way of moving through complexity, especially when prediction breaks down.

NOVA-U doesn't replace that insight. It supports it. It gives leaders a way to say, "This is where we are. This is what the context is asking of us." It also protects against the opposite risk of overcorrecting. Of thinking that because effectuation works in uncertain spaces, it must always be better. That's not what this model is about. And it's not what multi-dimensional leadership calls for.

Multi-dimensional leadership asks for discernment. It asks for awareness. It asks for leaders who can name the context, read the moment, and switch between reasoning styles without losing themselves, or their teams, in the process.

That's why NOVA-U belongs here. It's not just a framework. It's a compass. One that makes it easier to notice where you are, to choose your stance, and to carry others with you through the shift.

In some ways, it's the most practical expression of everything this book has been trying to surface: that leadership is not about mastering a single method. It's about learning how to move between them. To stay rooted in purpose while remaining flexible in approach. And to help others do the same by prioritizing presence, transparency, and care over expertise and theory.

That's where this work comes alive. Not just in theory, but in practice. Not just in what you choose to do, but in how you choose to do it, and when.

LEARNING TO SHIFT WITH PURPOSE

What this chapter has been circling, in many ways, is already familiar to most experienced leaders. The feeling of knowing that something isn't quite working because the context has changed. The sense that your usual instincts don't quite fit the moment you're in. That pause where you wonder if maybe it's not just the strategy that needs to shift, but the way you're reasoning through it.

That's the work of logic-switching. It sits quietly at the core of what I've come to call multi-dimensional leadership.

This isn't about having all the answers. It's about learning how to carry more than one lens. More than one method. It's about knowing when to trust the structure and when to let go of it. When to follow the map, and when to pay closer attention to the terrain under your feet.

Sometimes you lead by prediction. Sometimes you lead by control. And sometimes you lead by naming that the logic itself is what needs to change.

Over time, I've come to believe that this ability to notice, shift, and explain the shift to others isn't just a technique. It's a kind of maturity. It's a sign that leadership has deepened. It's no longer about defending your preferred tools, but about choosing the right ones for the moment at hand.

In the classroom, this idea often shows up in quiet ways. A student will say, "I've always defaulted to planning. I thought that's what made me a good leader." And then something shifts. They see how they've been waiting for clarity when maybe the moment called for motion. Or they realize they've been trying to force iteration into a space that needs structure. In that moment, something clicks. Not because they've abandoned what they know, but because they've added to it.

In organizations, I see the same thing. A leader comes to recognize that their strength, the thing they've always been known for, is only part of the picture. What made them effective in one season might need to stretch or loosen in the next. That's not a failure. It's growth.

So as you think about your own leadership, maybe the question isn't which logic you prefer. Maybe the question is: "Do you know how to shift when the moment calls for something else?"

If that question feels hard to answer, that's okay. Most of us weren't taught to think this way. But once you begin to notice the shift, once you start seeing the signals and giving them names, the terrain starts to change. You're not guessing anymore, you're navigating. With a compass that's not just internal, but shared. One that helps you move and helps others move with you.

That's what this chapter is offering. Not a prescription. Not a formula. Just a way to see more clearly what you're already doing, and maybe a way to do it with a little more intention. A little more care.

Because in the end, leadership is rarely about knowing what comes next. It's about knowing how to move when the next thing isn't clear and sometimes, that begins with the reasoning underneath it.

So pause. Notice. Name the compass.

And then, keep going.

A LIFE LIVED:

The Pressure to Predict - And The Cost Of Certainty

In the early days of the COVID-19 pandemic, no one had solid ground to stand on. We didn't know how the virus worked. We didn't know how it spread. We didn't know what would help or what would hurt.

Most leaders, national, local, organizational, were operating in a space with almost no validated data, no reliable precedent, and very little clarity about what to expect next.

For a little while, there was this small but meaningful pause. A moment when the uncertainty was named out loud. Some officials leaned into an effectual posture. They started with what they had. They ran pilots. They paid attention to early signals. They made decisions slowly, publicly, and with a posture of learning.

But that didn't last long.

Because the discomfort of that posture, of not knowing, not predicting, was too great. Public pressure mounted. People wanted answers. The media wanted headlines. Elected officials wanted control. Gradually, and then all at once, we shifted into a more causal mode.

Plans were drawn up. Forecasts were made. Graphs and models were shared widely. There was a confidence in those presentations, even when the data behind them was thin or incomplete. But the real shift wasn't just technical, it was psychological.

The research tells us that when people encounter uncertainty, the amygdala, the part of the brain associated with fear, activates. We start looking for patterns. For signals of safety. Causal reasoning offers that. It makes things feel more orderly. More answerable. Even when they're not.

That's what happened on a national scale. We defaulted to the logic that made us feel better, not necessarily the one the moment required.

And the outcomes showed it.

Across the United States, response strategies were largely structured as if the virus followed predictable rules. We tried to project timelines. We tried to set rigid thresholds. We built dashboards as if the underlying data had stability. When the virus didn't follow those patterns, trust started to erode and not just in the data, it eroded for the people sharing it.

Part of the challenge was that no one named the logic shift. That's what often makes leadership so difficult in these moments. The public was hearing a causal promise; charts, projections, delivery dates, but living through an effectual reality, where every week brought new variables.

There was no translation between those two logics. No acknowledgment that we had left one kind of reasoning behind and entered another. And when leaders don't help people make that transition, the result is confusion. Or worse, a quiet sense that something's not being said.

This is where the absence of sense-making became so visible across institutions and not just among policymakers. In high uncertainty environments, people don't just look for answers, they look for someone to help them make sense of what they're experiencing. They didn't need to resolve the tension immediately, they needed to name it. To stay with it. To hold enough structure that others can think clearly.

But in many cases, leaders didn't do that. They bypassed the discomfort, and in doing so, they skipped the deeper work of interpretation.

Sense-making isn't about controlling the narrative. It's about holding it open long enough that others can see themselves in it. That's what many systems failed to do. They defaulted to information rather than shared meaning. They offered clarity where coherence was needed. That kind of mismatch weakens trust through misalignment.

But not everyone made that shift.

Some countries, and even some U.S. states, chose to hold the effectual posture longer. They framed decisions as provisional. They invited front-line voices into the process. They moved with more humility and less certainty. In many of those places, outcomes were better. It wasn't that they made better predictions, it was that they trusted less in prediction and more in presence. They let learning shape the path.

They made room for collective interpretation. They didn't rush to say, "Here's the solution." They started by saying, "Here's what we're seeing, here's what we're learning, and here's what we're trying next."

That's what sense-making can sound like. It creates enough structure to move, but not so much that the system locks in prematurely. It invites others to stay involved as participants in meaning other than as passive recipients of information.

In hindsight, it's easy to see that what mattered wasn't just the decision-making, it was how the reasoning was held and whether others could see it. In places where leaders communicated their logic openly, where they translated between systems of thinking, and where they stayed close to frontline knowledge, trust held longer.

That kind of leadership isn't glamorous. It's not always popular. But it's what interpretive leaders do. They sense the kind of logic the moment calls for. They build coherence, even when certainty isn't available. They earn trust by being transparent, responsive, and anchored in something deeper than forecasts or by being right.

I think about that a lot now. Not because I think the wrong choices were made intentionally, but because they were made reflexively. We reached for the familiar tool instead of the right one. In doing so, we missed a different kind of opportunity.

Because uncertainty wasn't the enemy.

It was the environment.

PUTTING IT TO WORK: THREE DIMENSIONS OF APPLICATION

Industry

If you're leading a company, especially in a time of change, it can be easy to cling to what has worked before. Plans, forecasts, models. Sometimes those still hold.

But when the environment starts moving faster than your assumptions, logic-switching becomes less of a skill and more of a necessity. You might need to name, out loud, that the logic itself is shifting. That you're stepping from planning into exploration. That you're not abandoning structure, you're adapting it.

The teams around you may not have words for this. But they'll feel it. If you can help them see the shift, even in simple terms, it builds trust. It invites participation. It signals that leadership isn't just about pushing through. Sometimes, it's about paying attention to the kind of reasoning the moment needs.

Professional Career

Inside a career, especially as you take on more responsibility, there will be times when the skills that got you here won't be the ones that help you grow into what's next. You may be known for being decisive or thoughtful, or for making a tight plan and sticking to it.

That might still serve you, but if you start noticing that things aren't moving, or that your instincts feel mismatched, it might be a sign that the reasoning underneath your choices needs to shift. This doesn't mean abandoning who you are. It means noticing what the moment is asking for, and being willing to stretch into it. When you do, you might find that your influence expands because you're working from a logic that fits.

Personal Life

This kind of awareness isn't limited to professional spaces. In life, too, we move through seasons where what once worked starts to feel a little off.

Maybe you've always solved things by planning ahead. Or maybe you've always trusted your gut and adjusted as you went.

Neither is wrong. But sometimes the situation changes. A relationship shifts. A health issue emerges. A new responsibility enters. The usual ways of making sense start to feel thin.

Those are often moments where it's not the answer that needs to change, it's the way you're reasoning. Just asking yourself, quietly, *Am I trying to predict something I can't?* or *Am I avoiding structure when it might actually help?* can open a little space. That space may be just enough to try a new move, or to notice a different way forward.

EPILOGUE
CROSSING THE STREAM

There's no real ending to a book like this. Not in the way most books end. No final insight, no clean wrap-up, no step-by-step. Just a pause. A breath. A place to stop for a moment and look around.

If you've come this far, you've probably already noticed this book was not trying to deliver answers. It was trying to reflect something. Something I've seen in rooms full of complexity, in leaders trying to find their footing, and in myself, usually not when things were clear, but when they weren't.

Leadership, at least the kind I've come to trust, doesn't begin with knowing. It begins with noticing. And then choosing. Choosing how to move, what to hold, when to step forward, and when to wait. Over time, those choices start to form a pattern. A way of showing up. Something deeper than style. Closer to a stance.

What I've tried to offer is a way of recognizing that stance. I've called it multi-dimensional leadership. But I want to be clear; this is not a label and a new model to adopt. It's a lens. A way of noticing what you're already doing, and how to strengthen it. A way of understanding how we lead through complexity by learning to hold it and not by avoiding the tension. To work within it. To lead across it.

That's not simple work. And it doesn't come with a script.

But it does have tools. Part of what I want to name, especially here at the end, is that at the center of multi-dimensional leadership is something very concrete. Something that's often hidden underneath the surface of our decisions: the ability to move between two fundamental ways of thinking.

Leadership doesn't always look like leadership. It doesn't always start with clarity or direction. Sometimes it begins the way this story begins, with motion. With stepping into something you didn't entirely choose. Noticing that people are watching you differently, even though you're just doing the next thing that needs to be done.

This chapter isn't about a model or a moment. It's about how identity takes shape through uncertainty. And how, over time, the choices we make, especially the ones that don't feel like choices at the time, start to form a kind of throughline. Not a clean one. Not always a visible one. But a thread that holds.

I've collected a lot of dots over the years, not just through work, but across a life that didn't move in a straight line. It has felt, at times, more like crossing a stream than following a path. No clear direction, just one rock at a time, sometimes steady and sometimes not, each one offering a place to stand for a while.

I used to think the important part was finding the right path. But looking back, I've come to believe something else. The movement itself is what matters.

Every step we take, especially the ones that don't feel strategic or visible or finished, leaves something behind. A lived experience. A moment that taught us something, even if we didn't see it at the time. Those moments become the dots. Not because we planned them that way, but because we were willing to move. Sometimes in uncertainty. Sometimes, just because something needed doing. And later, through reflection, we begin to see how those dots hold shape. How they carry us. How they begin to form a kind of logic we didn't know we were living into.

When I was young, I played sports. I served as an altar boy. I worked in my parents' camera shop, helping customers, handling film, and getting to know what it meant to show up for a family business.

I tried the trumpet, though it didn't stick. Golf did. I still play. School was hard. I wasn't a strong student. I got disciplined more times than I care to count. I struggled all the way through until graduate school. Failed accounting (twice). Started things I didn't finish. Drifted when I should've pushed.

But I kept showing up. Even when I wasn't sure why. Even when I didn't know what it would add up to. Eventually, something in me started to click. Somewhere in all of that, I found my way into the language of cash flow and financial statements. And now, somehow, that's become something I'm known for.

I didn't know any of it would matter. I wasn't tracking toward a goal. I was just doing what felt interesting. What gave me motion. What made me useful. I wasn't on stage. I wasn't in the band. I was usually off to the side, taking pictures. Watching. Picking things up. I learned to cook from my grandmother and mom, mostly without recipes. I learned how to work on engines. How to do bodywork. I laid brick. Wired walls. Patched roofs. Learned to run a bar. I made my first sale when I was eight. Did my first solo sales call at fifteen. Bought real estate early. Some deals worked. Others didn't. A lot of the lessons came the hard way. But they came.

THE EARLY DOTS

I didn't have a script. I wasn't tracking toward a leadership role. But looking back, I can see now that leadership was already taking shape, but not through a title, through behavior. Through choosing responsibility. Through learning how to carry weight and how to be useful. Even when I didn't see it that way, I was slowly becoming someone others could count on.

If there was a play unfolding, I didn't know the lines. But I had a sense, however faint, of how I wanted the story to end. I wanted it to mean something. I wanted it to be good.

Over time, as the scenes changed and new characters entered, a different ending revealed itself. One that was deeper than the one I first imagined. One that used every misstep, every moment of grace, every forgotten line, and every person who gave me a foothold.

That's what Multi-Dimensional Leadership feels like, at least to me. It's not rigid. It's not linear. It's not driven by an unchanging plan. It's more like setting a direction lightly but loosely enough to stay open to what might emerge and grounded enough to know what you stand for. You don't abandon the goal. You evolve it. And sometimes, what emerges is better than anything you could've architected at the start.

SHAPED BY PEOPLE, NOT PLANS

Later on, I became a founding partner in a venture capital fund. I've taught in twenty-two countries. Worked across five continents. I've embedded with Army civil affairs teams in Djibouti, helping entrepreneurs figure out how to build something of their own. I've worked with veterans, underrepresented groups, and people with disabilities, trying to create conditions where more people can take a real shot. I've taught on military bases around the world. I've even swum with great white sharks.

None of it unfolded cleanly. There were businesses that blew up and ideas that never landed. Relationships I didn't handle well. Opportunities I misread or didn't rise to. There were years when I was moving without much clarity. Doing things I cared about, but not really knowing where it was leading. I doubted myself. I felt fear. And still, I moved.

When I see old friends, especially ones who knew me back in high school or college, the thing they come back to, more than anything, is that I'm now a professor at an Ivy League university.

It always gets a laugh. They didn't mean to be disrespectful, they just remember the me that existed before all this. Before the degrees. Before the credibility. Before I looked like someone with answers. They remember the version that was still stumbling through it. I remember that version too.

There have been so many people who helped me find the next rock in the stream. Some gave me a push. Some reached out and pulled. Some just stood next to me until I was ready to move on my own.

My dad taught me about business and what it means to belong to a community. These were lessons I didn't learn from books and could not learn in business school, but lessons I learned from watching him live them. But it wasn't just that he taught me. He was my first and most consistent thinking partner. My best friend, in a lot of ways. The person I could always go to when I needed to think something through. He'd push back, and sometimes it was hard for me to hear. He didn't just nod along. He asked questions I hadn't considered. He challenged assumptions. He helped me see what I wasn't seeing yet. And even when I didn't like what he said, I trusted it because I knew it came from care.

He didn't just teach me how business works, instead, he used business to show me life. How people move. What they need. What they notice. What they overlook. For him, business wasn't just a profession; it had meaning. It was a lens for understanding the world and being useful in it. And that lens became part of how I see things too.

My mom taught me that the world is full of possibility. How to treat people with dignity. How to move through life with humility, even when things are hard. She also shaped something deeper in me, something moral and internal. My time as an altar boy and the faith that took root in those years helped form that foundation.

But it was my wife, more than anyone, who deepened it. She has a way of seeing the world that's steady and principled, and over the years, that steadiness has shaped me too. Her influence helped clarify what I believe in and what I stand for. Together, those experiences gave shape to my moral compass, my ethical boundaries, and my sense of what's right. More than once, when the stream felt wide or unclear, it was those quiet inner bearings that pointed the way.

Through all of the missteps, failures, and moments in which I couldn't see a way forward, my mom and dad were there. Sometimes with a gentle word. Sometimes with a firmer hand. But always with the same intent: to help me find my way through. They didn't push me to a path of their own creation. They didn't try to protect me from failure. They helped me walk through it.

Over time, that changed how I understood what failure even was. Failure is just part of the journey, and it isn't something to avoid or be ashamed of. A place where something can be learned as you pass through on the way to something better. They never framed it as a weakness. They framed it as movement. As growth. As something I could survive and sometimes even be shaped by.

My sisters helped me see what it means to be a woman in this world, not as an abstract idea, but through real moments and conversations that challenged and changed me. And my son has reawakened something in me that I genuinely thought I had lost. Not because I stopped believing in it, but because life got full. Responsibilities took up more space. That part of me that used to chase new ideas just to see where they led started to fade into the background.

But watching him now as he takes risks, builds things from scratch, and lets himself get curious without overthinking it is bringing something back to the surface for me. That creative energy. That forward pull. That sense that something new is always possible if we're willing to lean in and try.

He reminds me, by the way he moves through the world, that possibility never really disappears. It just waits. It waits for us to remember it. To re-engage with it. To let it matter again. In doing that, he's not just shaping his future, he's reshaping mine by helping me remember something I already knew. Something I'd let sit for a while. Building something, trying something, dreaming about what could be is not just for the young. It's for anyone who's still willing to care. Still willing to start.

My best friend and I shared some of the brightest parts of my early life. We laughed hard and often, but we also walked through something we weren't ready for. A loss that didn't belong to us because it was his to carry. It came too fast, and we were too young. It changed us in ways we didn't fully understand back then. We were still boys, and yet we had to grow up fast and, in that moment, he somehow let me carry a little of it with him for a while. It was a privilege, and that kind of trust changes you. It teaches you how to be near pain without trying to fix it. It teaches you what it means to just stay close.

Even now, so many years later, he's still one of the people I hold closest because of that moment in time. Because of the way he let me walk beside him when everything was broken open.

So many people. So many dots. So much love. And more than enough grief. All of it lives in me, and all of it has helped shape the place I'm standing in now. The leader I have become.

When I look at the whole of it, I don't see a path. Not in the traditional sense. There's no map. No clean story. It's more like a stream I've been crossing one rock at a time.

It wasn't a strategy in the formal sense. It was something closer to what I now know as effectual thinking, the idea that we move not by predicting the future, but by using what's in our hands to create it. At the time, I didn't have a name for it; I just knew that motion mattered. That showing up mattered. That one rock might lead to the next, even if I couldn't see where it was all heading.

Each job, each relationship, each mistake, each person who gave me a chance, all of it was just the next rock. Some were steady. Some were slippery. Some I missed and had to circle back.

I got my feet wet more than once, but I kept moving toward the next solid place to stand instead of toward a fixed goal. The next thing I could learn from. The next thing I could contribute to. Somehow, across enough time, those rocks brought me here. To this work. To this classroom. To this role. A place that, for now, feels like it fits. Not because it was part of a plan, but because it makes use of all of it. The pictures. The problems. The lessons. The failures. All the lived experience.

If I've grown into anything, it's not because I picked a lane early or followed a clean arc. It's because I stayed in motion. I let myself become a combination of things: the builder, the teacher, the entrepreneur, the friend, the son. I didn't try to force it into one identity. I let the dimensions layer.

Now, more often than not, I find that what I've lived through is exactly what someone else needs. That's the strange gift of it. The very things that felt scattered at the time allow me to show up fully now.

THE DIRECTION THAT TOOK SHAPE

That's what this part of the journey is about for me now. That I might be a rock in someone else's stream. A steady place to stand for a while. A dot that hasn't yet connected. I don't need to be remembered. I just want to be useful. If even one student or corporate leader sees something differently because of our time together, if something I share becomes a foothold when they're finding their way, then that's enough, and I will claim success.

Here's the truth I've come to believe: this way of moving, this accumulation of dots, this responsiveness to what emerges, isn't just a personal story. It's a leadership stance. In every organization I've worked with, especially at the executive level, the same pattern holds. The best leaders aren't always the ones who executed the cleanest plan. They're the ones who stayed present and flexible. Who knew how to re-anchor when things shifted. They could take what they had, make something of it, and invite others to do the same.

You can see it in companies like Lamborghini. Originally a tractor manufacturer that pivoted into high-performance cars because of a founder's frustration with a Ferrari clutch on his tractor, and a willingness to follow what emerged. There was never a long-range plan, just movement. That one move, grounded in experience, not prediction, changed the entire trajectory of the brand.

You can see it in Marriott, which began as a root beer stand and evolved into one of the most recognized names in global hospitality. The journey wasn't linear. It was effectual. Adaptive. Built on moments of usefulness and insight.

That's what makes an organization resilient. That's what allows people to grow inside systems instead of being constrained by them. In the end, institutions don't move because of policies. They move because of people, and especially the people willing to lead in ways that are real, adaptive, and grounded in experience.

So while this reflection may sound personal, it's also a call to notice the dots you're gathering, the rocks you're stepping onto, and the way your leadership is shaping not just outcomes, but lives.

When I look back at all of it now, all these dots that make me who I am, I can see that none of them came from a job title, a degree, or a big achievement. They came from people. Not from a text. Not from a short video. Every meaningful moment in my story was shaped by someone. A parent. A student. A friend. A teacher. A dean. A stranger.

In the work I do now, I often talk about helping others find their compass, something internal they can trust when the way forward isn't obvious. But my own compass didn't emerge in isolation. It was shaped by those same dots. It came from the people who challenged me, stood by me, and loved me. The people who showed up just when I needed them most. My direction wasn't found alone. It was formed in relationships.

It wasn't institutions that changed me. It was conversation. It was presence. It was the way someone showed up at just the right time.

Maybe that's the part we forget too easily. The rocks in our streams and the places we stand, the ones that hold us steady, aren't things we build alone.

They're placed there, often, through interaction. Through connection. Through being part of the world in a real way and not through screens, feeds, or constant distraction, but through the actual friction and grace of being with people. In the room. In the work. In each other's lives.

That's where the meaning lives. That's where the next step comes from.

I'm not someone who spends much time looking back. There's no value in reliving things I can't change. But every so often, I'll glance in the rearview, not to second-guess, just to understand the shape of the road. What it taught me. What it gave me. What it asked of me.

Somewhere along the way, I learned this: if you build a good compass, know what matters, and stay anchored to it, the path will keep pulling you toward growth. Toward becoming a better version of yourself or a better future for your company. Not always smoothly. Not always quickly. But forward.

That doesn't mean the uncertainty goes away. It just means it stops being so paralyzing. Once you trust your compass, you don't have to see the whole road to take the next step. That's true in a company. It's true in a career. And it's true in a life lived.

But I don't think my stream is done. I haven't yet reached the other side. I don't think this is the final crossing. I'm sure there's another move coming. Another rock I haven't seen yet. Something that's not visible but will be.

When it shows up, I hope I'll still be paying attention. Still open. Still stepping and hopping. Still willing to move, even if the shape of it doesn't look like the plan.

What I am leaving you with is not a map or a playbook, it's just a reminder that you're already in motion, and motion is enough. In your organization, that might mean staying open to what emerges even when the strategy shifts.

In your career, it might mean trusting the value of what you've lived, even when it doesn't fit the mold.

And in your life, it might just mean remembering you're allowed to keep becoming. Growth doesn't stop. Leadership, real leadership, starts wherever you are and with whatever's in your hands.

Maybe, in the last moments of this book, you might reflect on your stream. Not to figure it all out, but just to notice. What have you stood on? What moments carried you, even if they didn't seem important at the time? What conversations, decisions, failures, or patterns quietly shaped who you are now?

You don't need to name all the dots. But you might start to see that they're there. That you've been building something. That you've been leading, maybe longer than you thought.

If you're still showing up, still moving through the unknown, still holding what matters, you're already becoming a multi-dimensional leader.

Keep going. Keep noticing. The next dot might already be forming.

THE RESEARCH THAT MADE THIS POSSIBLE

None of this would have come into focus without the work of others. It feels important to say that clearly.

I didn't invent effectuation. I learned it through the work of Saras Sarasvathy, whose research opened a door that had been sitting right in front of me for years. Her lens gave structure to instincts I had lived, but didn't yet have language for. That insight didn't just explain how entrepreneurs move through uncertainty; it helped me see my path differently. And it became a cornerstone of how I teach, coach, and lead.

But her work was just one part of a broader landscape. Researchers across disciplines like organizational behavior, decision theory, complexity science, leadership psychology, they've all left pieces of the puzzle. What I've done is not create something new from scratch. What I've done is collect and connect what was already there. I've taken the scattered tools of practice and research and tried to show how they can live together. How they can be applied by real people in real systems.

That's always been my place. I am a practitioner, not a scholar. My role isn't to generate theory. It's to bring it to life. I turn to the research to help make sense of what I am living to help others apply it when the playbook starts to fall short. And over time, that back-and-forth began to clarify something. It gave shape to what I now call multi-dimensional leadership.

So if this book holds any clarity, any pattern worth noticing, it's because others laid the groundwork. Their studies. Their questions. Their frameworks. I owe them a great deal and I hope this contribution does what they made possible, to carry those insights into rooms where they can move people, not just ideas.

NO FINISH LINE

What I hope you've found in these pages is not a final answer, but a way of naming what you already know to be true: leadership doesn't always look like certainty. It's not about having the perfect plan. It's about being in motion. Staying responsive. Staying human.

I don't think there's a finish line to this kind of leadership. There's just the next moment. The next decision. The next tension to hold with care.

You don't need to master both logics overnight. You don't need to resolve the ambiguity. You just need to stay in it. Keep noticing. Keep choosing how to move based on what's real, not what's ideal.

If you're doing that, you're already further along than you think.

So I'll leave you with this:

There's nothing wrong with prediction. And there's nothing weak about not knowing. What matters is how you show up when the world won't sit still. What matters is whether you can move between knowing and listening, planning and responding, and leading with conviction and care.

What matters is whether you're willing to keep becoming. Not into something better, just into something more fully yourself.

Because, in the end, that's what this book is really about.

Not leadership in the abstract.

But leadership, as it's lived.

One decision at a time.

A NOTE ON PROCESS

The ideas in this book come from decades of lived experience, working across systems, teaching inside complexity, listening to scholars, and walking alongside leaders as they navigate real change. The stories, frameworks, and reflections are drawn from that lived ground.

As I worked to give these ideas their clearest shape, I used the same tools I encourage others to explore. That includes generative AI, which I used at various points to help refine language, smooth transitions, and clarify structure.

But the thinking, the models, and the core voice are my own. What you've read reflects the accumulated weight of years in the work; not a script, but a synthesis.

I chose to share this because part of leadership today involves learning how to work with new tools without outsourcing the things that matter most, and that includes authorship.

SOURCES

Antonovsky, Aaron. 1987. *Unraveling the Mystery of Health: How People Manage Stress and Stay Well.* San Francisco: Jossey-Bass. (Chapter 4)

Argyris, Chris. 1991. "Teaching Smart People How to Learn." *Harvard Business Review* 69(3): 99–109. (Chapters 2, 3)

Ashforth, Blake E., and Ronald H. Humphrey. 1993. "Emotional Labor in Service Roles: The Influence of Identity." *Academy of Management Review* 18(1): 88–115. (Chapter 6)

Christensen, Clayton M., James Allworth, and Karen Dillon. 2012. *How Will You Measure Your Life?* New York: Harper Business. (Chapters 5, 10)

Dane, Erik, and Michael G. Pratt. 2007. "Exploring Intuition and Its Role in Managerial Decision Making." *Academy of Management Review* 32(1): 33–54. (Chapter 5)

Deloitte. 2021. *Global Human Capital Trends: The Social Enterprise in a World Disrupted.* Deloitte Insights. https://www2.deloitte.com (Chapter 8)

Detert, James R., and Amy C. Edmondson. 2011. "Implicit Voice Theories: Taken-for-Granted Rules of Self-Censorship at Work." *Academy of Management Journal* 54(3): 461–488. (Chapter 6)

Dervin, Brenda. 1998. "Sense-Making Theory and Practice: An Overview of User Interests in Knowledge Seeking and Use." *Journal of Knowledge Management* 2(2): 36–46. (Chapter 4)

Dörner, Dietrich. 1996. *The Logic of Failure: Recognizing and Avoiding Error in Complex Situations.* New York: Basic Books. (Chapter 9)

Edmondson, Amy C. 1999. "Psychological Safety and Learning Behavior in Work Teams." *Administrative Science Quarterly* 44(2): 350–383. (Chapters 3, 4, 5, 6, 9)

Ethisphere. 2022. *World's Most Ethical Companies: Insights Report.* https://www.ethisphere.com/resources/worlds-most-ethical-companies/ (Chapter 8)

EY Global. 2022. *Global Integrity Report 2022: Is Your Organization Living Up to Its Values?* https://www.ey.com/en_gl/assurance/global-integrity-report (Chapter 8)

Gavetti, Giovanni, and Daniel Levinthal. 2000. "Looking Forward and Looking Backward: Cognitive and Experiential Search." *Administrative Science Quarterly* 45(1): 113–137. (Chapter 5)

Gigerenzer, Gerd. 2007. *Gut Feelings: The Intelligence of the Unconscious.* New York: Viking. (Chapter 9)

Grant, Adam M. 2013. *Give and Take: A Revolutionary Approach to Success.* New York: Viking. (Chapter 6)

Harvard Business School. 2015. "Toxic Workers." HBS Working Paper No. 16-057. https://www.hbs.edu/faculty/Pages/item.aspx?num=49684 (Chapter 8)

Heifetz, Ronald A., and Marty Linsky. 2002. *Leadership on the Line: Staying Alive Through the Dangers of Leading.* Boston: Harvard Business Review Press. (Chapters 2, 3, 6)

Ibarra, Herminia. 2015. *Act Like a Leader, Think Like a Leader.* Boston: Harvard Business Review Press. (Chapter 6)

Hannah, Sean T., Bruce J. Avolio, and Fred O. Walumbwa. 2014. "Moral Identity and Leader Behavior: A Meta-Analytic Review." *Journal of Applied Psychology* 99(2): 261–281. (Chapter 8)

Kahneman, Daniel. 2011. *Thinking, Fast and Slow.* New York: Farrar, Straus and Giroux. (Chapters 1, 2, 3, 5, 9)

Kahneman, Daniel, and Amos Tversky. 1979. "Prospect Theory: An Analysis of Decision under Risk." *Econometrica* 47(2): 263–291. (Chapter 1)

Kahneman, Daniel, and Gary Klein. 2009. "Conditions for Intuitive Expertise: A Failure to Disagree." *American Psychologist* 64(6): 515–526. (Chapter 9)

Klein, Gary. 1998. *Sources of Power: How People Make Decisions.* Cambridge, MA: MIT Press. (Chapters 4, 5, 9, 10)

Levinthal, Daniel A., and James G. March. 1993. "The Myopia of Learning." *Strategic Management Journal* 14(S2): 95–112. (Chapters 5, 7, 10)

Maitlis, Sally, and Marlys Christianson. 2014. "Sensemaking in Organizations: Taking Stock and Moving Forward." *Academy of Management Annals* 8(1): 57–125. (Chapter 4)

March, James G. 1991. "Exploration and Exploitation in Organizational Learning." *Organization Science* 2(1): 71–87. (Chapters 1, 2)

McGrath, Rita Gunther, and Ian MacMillan. 2000. *The Entrepreneurial Mindset: Strategies for Continuously Creating Opportunity in an Age of Uncertainty.* Boston: Harvard Business School Press. (Chapter 7)

McKinsey & Company. 2021. *Strategic Planning in Volatile Times: Survey Insights from 1,200 Global Executives.* https://www.mckinsey.com/business-functions/strategy-and-corporate-finance/our-insights/strategic-planning-in-volatile-times (Chapter 10)

Mintzberg, Henry. 1994. *The Rise and Fall of Strategic Planning: Reconceiving Roles for Planning, Plans, Planners.* New York: Free Press. (Chapter 1)

Mintzberg, Henry. 2004. *Managers Not MBAs: A Hard Look at the Soft Practice of Managing and Management Development.* San Francisco: Berrett-Koehler. (Chapter 2)

Morrison, Elizabeth Wolfe. 2014. "Employee Voice and Silence." *Annual Review of Organizational Psychology and Organizational Behavior* 1(1): 173–197. (Chapter 6)

Ng, Thomas W. H., Daniel C. Feldman, and Christian Resick. 2015. "The Effects of Ethical Leadership on Burnout." *Organizational Behavior and Human Decision Processes* 126(1): 88–104. (Chapter 8)

O'Reilly, Charles A., and Michael L. Tushman. 2016. "Lead and Disrupt: How to Solve the Innovator's Dilemma." *California Management Review* 58(4): 50–76. (Chapter 6)

Polanyi, Michael. 1966. *The Tacit Dimension.* Garden City, NY: Doubleday. (Chapter 9)

Read, Stuart, Saras D. Sarasvathy, Nick Dew, Robert Wiltbank, and Anne-Valérie Ohlsson. 2011. *Effectual Entrepreneurship.* New York: Routledge. (Chapter 7)

Sarasvathy, Saras D. 2001. "Causation and Effectuation: Toward a Theoretical Shift from Economic Inevitability to Entrepreneurial Contingency." *Academy of Management Review* 26(2): 243–263. (Chapters 1, 2, 3, 5, 7, 10)

Sarasvathy, Saras D. 2008. *Effectuation: Elements of Entrepreneurial Expertise.* Cheltenham, UK: Edward Elgar Publishing. (Chapters 7, 9, 10)

Schein, Edgar H. 2010. *Organizational Culture and Leadership.* 4th ed. San Francisco: Jossey-Bass. (Chapters 5, 6, 7, 8, 10)

Schön, Donald A. 1983. *The Reflective Practitioner: How Professionals Think in Action.* New York: Basic Books. (Chapters 1, 2, 7, 10)

Simon, Herbert A. 1997. *Administrative Behavior: A Study of Decision-Making Processes in Administrative Organizations.* 4th ed. New York: Free Press. (Chapters 1, 3)

Simons, Tony. 2002. "The High Cost of Lost Trust: When Employees Don't Believe Their Leader." *Harvard Business Review* 80(9): 18–19. (Chapters 4, 5)

Trishul, K. *Dissertation in progress*, Mahindra University. Personal communication, 2024.

Tversky, Amos, and Daniel Kahneman. 1974. "Judgment under Uncertainty: Heuristics and Biases." *Science* 185(4157): 1124–1131. (Chapters 5, 9)

Tversky, Amos, and Daniel Kahneman. 1981. "The Framing of Decisions and the Psychology of Choice." *Science* 211(4481): 453–458. (Chapter 3)

Van Dyne, Linn, and Jeffrey LePine. 1998. "Helping and Voice Extra-Role Behaviors: Evidence of Construct and Predictive Validity." *Academy of Management Journal* 41(1): 108–119. (Chapter 6)

Weick, Karl E. 1995. *Sensemaking in Organizations.* Thousand Oaks, CA: Sage Publications. (Chapters 1–5, 7–10)

Weick, Karl E., Kathleen M. Sutcliffe, and David Obstfeld. 2005. "Organizing and the Process of Sensemaking." *Organization Science* 16(4): 409–421. (Chapter 10)

Woolley, Anita W., and Christopher F. Chabris. 2021. "Cognitive Framing Alignment and Team Adaptability in Uncertain Environments." *Organization Science* 32(6): 1293–1311. (Chapter 10)

THANK YOU FOR READING MY BOOK!

Step Into Multi-Dimensional Leadership

Thank you for reading *The Purposeful Leader*.
Download your free exclusive tools, including the NOVA-U
Framework, to help you bring these ideas to life.

Scan the QR code, no obligation, just actionable resources.

If you're interested in becoming a client and developing
multi-dimensional leadership skills for yourself or your
team, please use the link provided with your download.

Scan the QR Code:

*I appreciate your interest in my book and value your feedback as it helps me
improve future versions of this book. I would appreciate it if you could leave
your invaluable review on Amazon.com with your feedback. Thank you!*

www.ingramcontent.com/pod-product-compliance
Lightning Source LLC
Chambersburg PA
CBHW020154200326
41521CB00006B/364